C-173   CAREER EXAMINATION SERIES

This is your
PASSBOOK for...

Court Law Stenographer

Test Preparation Study Guide
Questions & Answers

COPYRIGHT NOTICE

This book is SOLELY intended for, is sold ONLY to, and its use is RESTRICTED to individual, bona fide applicants or candidates who qualify by virtue of having seriously filed applications for appropriate license, certificate, professional and/or promotional advancement, higher school matriculation, scholarship, or other legitimate requirements of education and/or governmental authorities.

This book is NOT intended for use, class instruction, tutoring, training, duplication, copying, reprinting, excerption, or adaptation, etc., by:

1) Other publishers
2) Proprietors and/or Instructors of "Coaching" and/or Preparatory Courses
3) Personnel and/or Training Divisions of commercial, industrial, and governmental organizations
4) Schools, colleges, or universities and/or their departments and staffs, including teachers and other personnel
5) Testing Agencies or Bureaus
6) Study groups which seek by the purchase of a single volume to copy and/or duplicate and/or adapt this material for use by the group as a whole without having purchased individual volumes for each of the members of the group
7) Et al.

Such persons would be in violation of appropriate Federal and State statutes.

PROVISION OF LICENSING AGREEMENTS – Recognized educational, commercial, industrial, and governmental institutions and organizations, and others legitimately engaged in educational pursuits, including training, testing, and measurement activities, may address request for a licensing agreement to the copyright owners, who will determine whether, and under what conditions, including fees and charges, the materials in this book may be used them. In other words, a licensing facility exists for the legitimate use of the material in this book on other than an individual basis. However, it is asseverated and affirmed here that the material in this book CANNOT be used without the receipt of the express permission of such a licensing agreement from the Publishers. Inquiries re licensing should be addressed to the company, attention rights and permissions department.

All rights reserved, including the right of reproduction in whole or in part, in any form or by any means, electronic or mechanical, including photocopying, recording, or by any information storage and retrieval system, without permission in writing from the Publisher.

Copyright © 2025 by
National Learning Corporation

212 Michael Drive, Syosset, NY 11791
(516) 921-8888 • www.passbooks.com
E-mail: info@passbooks.com

PASSBOOK® SERIES

THE *PASSBOOK® SERIES* has been created to prepare applicants and candidates for the ultimate academic battlefield – the examination room.

At some time in our lives, each and every one of us may be required to take an examination – for validation, matriculation, admission, qualification, registration, certification, or licensure.

Based on the assumption that every applicant or candidate has met the basic formal educational standards, has taken the required number of courses, and read the necessary texts, the *PASSBOOK® SERIES* furnishes the one special preparation which may assure passing with confidence, instead of failing with insecurity. Examination questions – together with answers – are furnished as the basic vehicle for study so that the mysteries of the examination and its compounding difficulties may be eliminated or diminished by a sure method.

This book is meant to help you pass your examination provided that you qualify and are serious in your objective.

The entire field is reviewed through the huge store of content information which is succinctly presented through a provocative and challenging approach – the question-and-answer method.

A climate of success is established by furnishing the correct answers at the end of each test.

You soon learn to recognize types of questions, forms of questions, and patterns of questioning. You may even begin to anticipate expected outcomes.

You perceive that many questions are repeated or adapted so that you can gain acute insights, which may enable you to score many sure points.

You learn how to confront new questions, or types of questions, and to attack them confidently and work out the correct answers.

You note objectives and emphases, and recognize pitfalls and dangers, so that you may make positive educational adjustments.

Moreover, you are kept fully informed in relation to new concepts, methods, practices, and directions in the field.

You discover that you are actually taking the examination all the time: you are preparing for the examination by "taking" an examination, not by reading extraneous and/or supererogatory textbooks.

In short, this PASSBOOK®, used directedly, should be an important factor in helping you to pass your test.

COURT LAW STENOGRAPHER

DUTIES
Performs stenographic and related duties in courtrooms during trials, hearings, and related proceedings. The work involves performing difficult specialized stenographic work involving the responsibility for taking and transcribing stenographic notes of verbatim testimony before a Grand Jury and at hearings, trials, interrogations and other proceedings involving two or more participants. Dictation is often taken at high rates of speed and under difficult conditions requiring the application of an unusually high degree of stenographic competence. Duties are performed according to specified procedures and completed transcriptions are examined by administrative and professional superiors for accuracy. Performs related work as required.

SCOPE OF THE EXAMINATION
The written test will cover knowledge, skills, and/or abilities in the following areas:
1. Reading comprehension;
2. Spelling;
3. Grammar and punctuation;
4. Preparing written material;
5. Proofreading; and
6. Keyboarding.

The performance test will require verbatim reporting of moderately difficult or technical two-voice dictation at the rate of 225 syllables per minute and transcribing that dictation with at least 95% accuracy. (The rate of 225 syllables per minute equals 160 to 180 words per minute, depending upon the syllabic density of the material.) The dictation will be presented on a video and will be in the form of a simulated hearing segment.

HOW TO TAKE A TEST

I. YOU MUST PASS AN EXAMINATION

A. WHAT EVERY CANDIDATE SHOULD KNOW

Examination applicants often ask us for help in preparing for the written test. What can I study in advance? What kinds of questions will be asked? How will the test be given? How will the papers be graded?

As an applicant for a civil service examination, you may be wondering about some of these things. Our purpose here is to suggest effective methods of advance study and to describe civil service examinations.

Your chances for success on this examination can be increased if you know how to prepare. Those "pre-examination jitters" can be reduced if you know what to expect. You can even experience an adventure in good citizenship if you know why civil service exams are given.

B. WHY ARE CIVIL SERVICE EXAMINATIONS GIVEN?

Civil service examinations are important to you in two ways. As a citizen, you want public jobs filled by employees who know how to do their work. As a job seeker, you want a fair chance to compete for that job on an equal footing with other candidates. The best-known means of accomplishing this two-fold goal is the competitive examination.

Exams are widely publicized throughout the nation. They may be administered for jobs in federal, state, city, municipal, town or village governments or agencies.

Any citizen may apply, with some limitations, such as the age or residence of applicants. Your experience and education may be reviewed to see whether you meet the requirements for the particular examination. When these requirements exist, they are reasonable and applied consistently to all applicants. Thus, a competitive examination may cause you some uneasiness now, but it is your privilege and safeguard.

C. HOW ARE CIVIL SERVICE EXAMS DEVELOPED?

Examinations are carefully written by trained technicians who are specialists in the field known as "psychological measurement," in consultation with recognized authorities in the field of work that the test will cover. These experts recommend the subject matter areas or skills to be tested; only those knowledges or skills important to your success on the job are included. The most reliable books and source materials available are used as references. Together, the experts and technicians judge the difficulty level of the questions.

Test technicians know how to phrase questions so that the problem is clearly stated. Their ethics do not permit "trick" or "catch" questions. Questions may have been tried out on sample groups, or subjected to statistical analysis, to determine their usefulness.

Written tests are often used in combination with performance tests, ratings of training and experience, and oral interviews. All of these measures combine to form the best-known means of finding the right person for the right job.

II. HOW TO PASS THE WRITTEN TEST

A. NATURE OF THE EXAMINATION

To prepare intelligently for civil service examinations, you should know how they differ from school examinations you have taken. In school you were assigned certain definite pages to read or subjects to cover. The examination questions were quite detailed and usually emphasized memory. Civil service exams, on the other hand, try to discover your present ability to perform the duties of a position, plus your potentiality to learn these duties. In other words, a civil service exam attempts to predict how successful you will be. Questions cover such a broad area that they cannot be as minute and detailed as school exam questions.

In the public service similar kinds of work, or positions, are grouped together in one "class." This process is known as *position-classification*. All the positions in a class are paid according to the salary range for that class. One class title covers all of these positions, and they are all tested by the same examination.

B. FOUR BASIC STEPS

1) Study the announcement

How, then, can you know what subjects to study? Our best answer is: "Learn as much as possible about the class of positions for which you've applied." The exam will test the knowledge, skills and abilities needed to do the work.

Your most valuable source of information about the position you want is the official exam announcement. This announcement lists the training and experience qualifications. Check these standards and apply only if you come reasonably close to meeting them.

The brief description of the position in the examination announcement offers some clues to the subjects which will be tested. Think about the job itself. Review the duties in your mind. Can you perform them, or are there some in which you are rusty? Fill in the blank spots in your preparation.

Many jurisdictions preview the written test in the exam announcement by including a section called "Knowledge and Abilities Required," "Scope of the Examination," or some similar heading. Here you will find out specifically what fields will be tested.

2) Review your own background

Once you learn in general what the position is all about, and what you need to know to do the work, ask yourself which subjects you already know fairly well and which need improvement. You may wonder whether to concentrate on improving your strong areas or on building some background in your fields of weakness. When the announcement has specified "some knowledge" or "considerable knowledge," or has used adjectives like "beginning principles of…" or "advanced … methods," you can get a clue as to the number and difficulty of questions to be asked in any given field. More questions, and hence broader coverage, would be included for those subjects which are more important in the work. Now weigh your strengths and weaknesses against the job requirements and prepare accordingly.

3) Determine the level of the position

Another way to tell how intensively you should prepare is to understand the level of the job for which you are applying. Is it the entering level? In other words, is this the position in which beginners in a field of work are hired? Or is it an intermediate or advanced level? Sometimes this is indicated by such words as "Junior" or "Senior" in the class title. Other jurisdictions use Roman numerals to designate the level – Clerk I, Clerk II, for example. The word "Supervisor" sometimes appears in the title. If the level is not indicated by the title, check the description of duties. Will you be working under very close supervision, or will you have responsibility for independent decisions in this work?

4) Choose appropriate study materials

Now that you know the subjects to be examined and the relative amount of each subject to be covered, you can choose suitable study materials. For beginning level jobs, or even advanced ones, if you have a pronounced weakness in some aspect of your training, read a modern, standard textbook in that field. Be sure it is up to date and has general coverage. Such books are normally available at your library, and the librarian will be glad to help you locate one. For entry-level positions, questions of appropriate difficulty are chosen – neither highly advanced questions, nor those too simple. Such questions require careful thought but not advanced training.

If the position for which you are applying is technical or advanced, you will read more advanced, specialized material. If you are already familiar with the basic principles of your field, elementary textbooks would waste your time. Concentrate on advanced textbooks and technical periodicals. Think through the concepts and review difficult problems in your field.

These are all general sources. You can get more ideas on your own initiative, following these leads. For example, training manuals and publications of the government agency which employs workers in your field can be useful, particularly for technical and professional positions. A letter or visit to the government department involved may result in more specific study suggestions, and certainly will provide you with a more definite idea of the exact nature of the position you are seeking.

III. KINDS OF TESTS

Tests are used for purposes other than measuring knowledge and ability to perform specified duties. For some positions, it is equally important to test ability to make adjustments to new situations or to profit from training. In others, basic mental abilities not dependent on information are essential. Questions which test these things may not appear as pertinent to the duties of the position as those which test for knowledge and information. Yet they are often highly important parts of a fair examination. For very general questions, it is almost impossible to help you direct your study efforts. What we can do is to point out some of the more common of these general abilities needed in public service positions and describe some typical questions.

1) General information

Broad, general information has been found useful for predicting job success in some kinds of work. This is tested in a variety of ways, from vocabulary lists to questions about current events. Basic background in some field of work, such as sociology or economics, may be sampled in a group of questions. Often these are principles which have become familiar to most persons through exposure rather than through formal training. It is difficult to advise you how to study for these questions; being alert to the world around you is our best suggestion.

2) Verbal ability

An example of an ability needed in many positions is verbal or language ability. Verbal ability is, in brief, the ability to use and understand words. Vocabulary and grammar tests are typical measures of this ability. Reading comprehension or paragraph interpretation questions are common in many kinds of civil service tests. You are given a paragraph of written material and asked to find its central meaning.

3) Numerical ability

Number skills can be tested by the familiar arithmetic problem, by checking paired lists of numbers to see which are alike and which are different, or by interpreting charts and graphs. In the latter test, a graph may be printed in the test booklet which you are asked to use as the basis for answering questions.

4) Observation

A popular test for law-enforcement positions is the observation test. A picture is shown to you for several minutes, then taken away. Questions about the picture test your ability to observe both details and larger elements.

5) Following directions

In many positions in the public service, the employee must be able to carry out written instructions dependably and accurately. You may be given a chart with several columns, each column listing a variety of information. The questions require you to carry out directions involving the information given in the chart.

6) Skills and aptitudes

Performance tests effectively measure some manual skills and aptitudes. When the skill is one in which you are trained, such as typing or shorthand, you can practice. These tests are often very much like those given in business school or high school courses. For many of the other skills and aptitudes, however, no short-time preparation can be made. Skills and abilities natural to you or that you have developed throughout your lifetime are being tested.

Many of the general questions just described provide all the data needed to answer the questions and ask you to use your reasoning ability to find the answers. Your best preparation for these tests, as well as for tests of facts and ideas, is to be at your physical and mental best. You, no doubt, have your own methods of getting into an exam-taking mood and keeping "in shape." The next section lists some ideas on this subject.

IV. KINDS OF QUESTIONS

Only rarely is the "essay" question, which you answer in narrative form, used in civil service tests. Civil service tests are usually of the short-answer type. Full instructions for answering these questions will be given to you at the examination. But in case this is your first experience with short-answer questions and separate answer sheets, here is what you need to know:

1) Multiple-choice Questions

Most popular of the short-answer questions is the "multiple choice" or "best answer" question. It can be used, for example, to test for factual knowledge, ability to solve problems or judgment in meeting situations found at work.

A multiple-choice question is normally one of three types—
- It can begin with an incomplete statement followed by several possible endings. You are to find the one ending which *best* completes the statement, although some of the others may not be entirely wrong.
- It can also be a complete statement in the form of a question which is answered by choosing one of the statements listed.

- It can be in the form of a problem – again you select the best answer.

Here is an example of a multiple-choice question with a discussion which should give you some clues as to the method for choosing the right answer:

When an employee has a complaint about his assignment, the action which will *best* help him overcome his difficulty is to
    A. discuss his difficulty with his coworkers
    B. take the problem to the head of the organization
    C. take the problem to the person who gave him the assignment
    D. say nothing to anyone about his complaint

In answering this question, you should study each of the choices to find which is best. Consider choice "A" – Certainly an employee may discuss his complaint with fellow employees, but no change or improvement can result, and the complaint remains unresolved. Choice "B" is a poor choice since the head of the organization probably does not know what assignment you have been given, and taking your problem to him is known as "going over the head" of the supervisor. The supervisor, or person who made the assignment, is the person who can clarify it or correct any injustice. Choice "C" is, therefore, correct. To say nothing, as in choice "D," is unwise. Supervisors have and interest in knowing the problems employees are facing, and the employee is seeking a solution to his problem.

2) True/False Questions

The "true/false" or "right/wrong" form of question is sometimes used. Here a complete statement is given. Your job is to decide whether the statement is right or wrong.

SAMPLE: A roaming cell-phone call to a nearby city costs less than a non-roaming call to a distant city.

This statement is wrong, or false, since roaming calls are more expensive.

This is not a complete list of all possible question forms, although most of the others are variations of these common types. You will always get complete directions for answering questions. Be sure you understand *how* to mark your answers – ask questions until you do.

V. RECORDING YOUR ANSWERS

Computer terminals are used more and more today for many different kinds of exams.

For an examination with very few applicants, you may be told to record your answers in the test booklet itself. Separate answer sheets are much more common. If this separate answer sheet is to be scored by machine – and this is often the case – it is highly important that you mark your answers correctly in order to get credit.

An electronic scoring machine is often used in civil service offices because of the speed with which papers can be scored. Machine-scored answer sheets must be marked with a pencil, which will be given to you. This pencil has a high graphite content which responds to the electronic scoring machine. As a matter of fact, stray dots may register as answers, so do not let your pencil rest on the answer sheet while you are pondering the correct answer. Also, if your pencil lead breaks or is otherwise defective, ask for another.

Since the answer sheet will be dropped in a slot in the scoring machine, be careful not to bend the corners or get the paper crumpled.

The answer sheet normally has five vertical columns of numbers, with 30 numbers to a column. These numbers correspond to the question numbers in your test booklet. After each number, going across the page are four or five pairs of dotted lines. These short dotted lines have small letters or numbers above them. The first two pairs may also have a "T" or "F" above the letters. This indicates that the first two pairs only are to be used if the questions are of the true-false type. If the questions are multiple choice, disregard the "T" and "F" and pay attention only to the small letters or numbers.

Answer your questions in the manner of the sample that follows:

32. The largest city in the United States is
   A. Washington, D.C.
   B. New York City
   C. Chicago
   D. Detroit
   E. San Francisco

1) Choose the answer you think is best. (New York City is the largest, so "B" is correct.)
2) Find the row of dotted lines numbered the same as the question you are answering. (Find row number 32)
3) Find the pair of dotted lines corresponding to the answer. (Find the pair of lines under the mark "B.")
4) Make a solid black mark between the dotted lines.

VI. BEFORE THE TEST

Common sense will help you find procedures to follow to get ready for an examination. Too many of us, however, overlook these sensible measures. Indeed, nervousness and fatigue have been found to be the most serious reasons why applicants fail to do their best on civil service tests. Here is a list of reminders:

- Begin your preparation early – Don't wait until the last minute to go scurrying around for books and materials or to find out what the position is all about.
- Prepare continuously – An hour a night for a week is better than an all-night cram session. This has been definitely established. What is more, a night a week for a month will return better dividends than crowding your study into a shorter period of time.
- Locate the place of the exam – You have been sent a notice telling you when and where to report for the examination. If the location is in a different town or otherwise unfamiliar to you, it would be well to inquire the best route and learn something about the building.
- Relax the night before the test – Allow your mind to rest. Do not study at all that night. Plan some mild recreation or diversion; then go to bed early and get a good night's sleep.
- Get up early enough to make a leisurely trip to the place for the test – This way unforeseen events, traffic snarls, unfamiliar buildings, etc. will not upset you.
- Dress comfortably – A written test is not a fashion show. You will be known by number and not by name, so wear something comfortable.

- Leave excess paraphernalia at home – Shopping bags and odd bundles will get in your way. You need bring only the items mentioned in the official notice you received; usually everything you need is provided. Do not bring reference books to the exam. They will only confuse those last minutes and be taken away from you when in the test room.
- Arrive somewhat ahead of time – If because of transportation schedules you must get there very early, bring a newspaper or magazine to take your mind off yourself while waiting.
- Locate the examination room – When you have found the proper room, you will be directed to the seat or part of the room where you will sit. Sometimes you are given a sheet of instructions to read while you are waiting. Do not fill out any forms until you are told to do so; just read them and be prepared.
- Relax and prepare to listen to the instructions
- If you have any physical problem that may keep you from doing your best, be sure to tell the test administrator. If you are sick or in poor health, you really cannot do your best on the exam. You can come back and take the test some other time.

VII. AT THE TEST

The day of the test is here and you have the test booklet in your hand. The temptation to get going is very strong. Caution! There is more to success than knowing the right answers. You must know how to identify your papers and understand variations in the type of short-answer question used in this particular examination. Follow these suggestions for maximum results from your efforts:

1) Cooperate with the monitor

The test administrator has a duty to create a situation in which you can be as much at ease as possible. He will give instructions, tell you when to begin, check to see that you are marking your answer sheet correctly, and so on. He is not there to guard you, although he will see that your competitors do not take unfair advantage. He wants to help you do your best.

2) Listen to all instructions

Don't jump the gun! Wait until you understand all directions. In most civil service tests you get more time than you need to answer the questions. So don't be in a hurry. Read each word of instructions until you clearly understand the meaning. Study the examples, listen to all announcements and follow directions. Ask questions if you do not understand what to do.

3) Identify your papers

Civil service exams are usually identified by number only. You will be assigned a number; you must not put your name on your test papers. Be sure to copy your number correctly. Since more than one exam may be given, copy your exact examination title.

4) Plan your time

Unless you are told that a test is a "speed" or "rate of work" test, speed itself is usually not important. Time enough to answer all the questions will be provided, but this does not mean that you have all day. An overall time limit has been set. Divide the total time (in minutes) by the number of questions to determine the approximate time you have for each question.

5) Do not linger over difficult questions

If you come across a difficult question, mark it with a paper clip (useful to have along) and come back to it when you have been through the booklet. One caution if you do this – be sure to skip a number on your answer sheet as well. Check often to be sure that you have not lost your place and that you are marking in the row numbered the same as the question you are answering.

6) Read the questions

Be sure you know what the question asks! Many capable people are unsuccessful because they failed to *read* the questions correctly.

7) Answer all questions

Unless you have been instructed that a penalty will be deducted for incorrect answers, it is better to guess than to omit a question.

8) Speed tests

It is often better NOT to guess on speed tests. It has been found that on timed tests people are tempted to spend the last few seconds before time is called in marking answers at random – without even reading them – in the hope of picking up a few extra points. To discourage this practice, the instructions may warn you that your score will be "corrected" for guessing. That is, a penalty will be applied. The incorrect answers will be deducted from the correct ones, or some other penalty formula will be used.

9) Review your answers

If you finish before time is called, go back to the questions you guessed or omitted to give them further thought. Review other answers if you have time.

10) Return your test materials

If you are ready to leave before others have finished or time is called, take ALL your materials to the monitor and leave quietly. Never take any test material with you. The monitor can discover whose papers are not complete, and taking a test booklet may be grounds for disqualification.

VIII. EXAMINATION TECHNIQUES

1) Read the general instructions carefully. These are usually printed on the first page of the exam booklet. As a rule, these instructions refer to the timing of the examination; the fact that you should not start work until the signal and must stop work at a signal, etc. If there are any *special* instructions, such as a choice of questions to be answered, make sure that you note this instruction carefully.

2) When you are ready to start work on the examination, that is as soon as the signal has been given, read the instructions to each question booklet, underline any key words or phrases, such as *least, best, outline, describe* and the like. In this way you will tend to answer as requested rather than discover on reviewing your paper that you *listed without describing*, that you selected the *worst* choice rather than the *best* choice, etc.

3) If the examination is of the objective or multiple-choice type – that is, each question will also give a series of possible answers: A, B, C or D, and you are called upon to select the best answer and write the letter next to that answer on your answer paper – it is advisable to start answering each question in turn. There may be anywhere from 50 to 100 such questions in the three or four hours allotted and you can see how much time would be taken if you read through all the questions before beginning to answer any. Furthermore, if you come across a question or group of questions which you know would be difficult to answer, it would undoubtedly affect your handling of all the other questions.

4) If the examination is of the essay type and contains but a few questions, it is a moot point as to whether you should read all the questions before starting to answer any one. Of course, if you are given a choice – say five out of seven and the like – then it is essential to read all the questions so you can eliminate the two that are most difficult. If, however, you are asked to answer all the questions, there may be danger in trying to answer the easiest one first because you may find that you will spend too much time on it. The best technique is to answer the first question, then proceed to the second, etc.

5) Time your answers. Before the exam begins, write down the time it started, then add the time allowed for the examination and write down the time it must be completed, then divide the time available somewhat as follows:
    - If 3-1/2 hours are allowed, that would be 210 minutes. If you have 80 objective-type questions, that would be an average of 2-1/2 minutes per question. Allow yourself no more than 2 minutes per question, or a total of 160 minutes, which will permit about 50 minutes to review.
    - If for the time allotment of 210 minutes there are 7 essay questions to answer, that would average about 30 minutes a question. Give yourself only 25 minutes per question so that you have about 35 minutes to review.

6) The most important instruction is to *read each question* and make sure you know what is wanted. The second most important instruction is to *time yourself properly* so that you answer every question. The third most important instruction is to *answer every question*. Guess if you have to but include something for each question. Remember that you will receive no credit for a blank and will probably receive some credit if you write something in answer to an essay question. If you guess a letter – say "B" for a multiple-choice question – you may have guessed right. If you leave a blank as an answer to a multiple-choice question, the examiners may respect your feelings but it will not add a point to your score. Some exams may penalize you for wrong answers, so in such cases *only*, you may not want to guess unless you have some basis for your answer.

7) Suggestions
    a. Objective-type questions
        1. Examine the question booklet for proper sequence of pages and questions
        2. Read all instructions carefully
        3. Skip any question which seems too difficult; return to it after all other questions have been answered
        4. Apportion your time properly; do not spend too much time on any single question or group of questions

5. Note and underline key words – *all, most, fewest, least, best, worst, same, opposite*, etc.
6. Pay particular attention to negatives
7. Note unusual option, e.g., unduly long, short, complex, different or similar in content to the body of the question
8. Observe the use of "hedging" words – *probably, may, most likely*, etc.
9. Make sure that your answer is put next to the same number as the question
10. Do not second-guess unless you have good reason to believe the second answer is definitely more correct
11. Cross out original answer if you decide another answer is more accurate; do not erase until you are ready to hand your paper in
12. Answer all questions; guess unless instructed otherwise
13. Leave time for review

    b. Essay questions
      1. Read each question carefully
      2. Determine exactly what is wanted. Underline key words or phrases.
      3. Decide on outline or paragraph answer
      4. Include many different points and elements unless asked to develop any one or two points or elements
      5. Show impartiality by giving pros and cons unless directed to select one side only
      6. Make and write down any assumptions you find necessary to answer the questions
      7. Watch your English, grammar, punctuation and choice of words
      8. Time your answers; don't crowd material

8) Answering the essay question

Most essay questions can be answered by framing the specific response around several key words or ideas. Here are a few such key words or ideas:

M's: manpower, materials, methods, money, management
P's: purpose, program, policy, plan, procedure, practice, problems, pitfalls, personnel, public relations
    a. Six basic steps in handling problems:
      1. Preliminary plan and background development
      2. Collect information, data and facts
      3. Analyze and interpret information, data and facts
      4. Analyze and develop solutions as well as make recommendations
      5. Prepare report and sell recommendations
      6. Install recommendations and follow up effectiveness

    b. Pitfalls to avoid
      1. *Taking things for granted* – A statement of the situation does not necessarily imply that each of the elements is necessarily true; for example, a complaint may be invalid and biased so that all that can be taken for granted is that a complaint has been registered

2. *Considering only one side of a situation* – Wherever possible, indicate several alternatives and then point out the reasons you selected the best one
3. *Failing to indicate follow up* – Whenever your answer indicates action on your part, make certain that you will take proper follow-up action to see how successful your recommendations, procedures or actions turn out to be
4. *Taking too long in answering any single question* – Remember to time your answers properly

IX. AFTER THE TEST

Scoring procedures differ in detail among civil service jurisdictions although the general principles are the same. Whether the papers are hand-scored or graded by machine we have described, they are nearly always graded by number. That is, the person who marks the paper knows only the number – never the name – of the applicant. Not until all the papers have been graded will they be matched with names. If other tests, such as training and experience or oral interview ratings have been given, scores will be combined. Different parts of the examination usually have different weights. For example, the written test might count 60 percent of the final grade, and a rating of training and experience 40 percent. In many jurisdictions, veterans will have a certain number of points added to their grades.

After the final grade has been determined, the names are placed in grade order and an eligible list is established. There are various methods for resolving ties between those who get the same final grade – probably the most common is to place first the name of the person whose application was received first. Job offers are made from the eligible list in the order the names appear on it. You will be notified of your grade and your rank as soon as all these computations have been made. This will be done as rapidly as possible.

People who are found to meet the requirements in the announcement are called "eligibles." Their names are put on a list of eligible candidates. An eligible's chances of getting a job depend on how high he stands on this list and how fast agencies are filling jobs from the list.

When a job is to be filled from a list of eligibles, the agency asks for the names of people on the list of eligibles for that job. When the civil service commission receives this request, it sends to the agency the names of the three people highest on this list. Or, if the job to be filled has specialized requirements, the office sends the agency the names of the top three persons who meet these requirements from the general list.

The appointing officer makes a choice from among the three people whose names were sent to him. If the selected person accepts the appointment, the names of the others are put back on the list to be considered for future openings.

That is the rule in hiring from all kinds of eligible lists, whether they are for typist, carpenter, chemist, or something else. For every vacancy, the appointing officer has his choice of any one of the top three eligibles on the list. This explains why the person whose name is on top of the list sometimes does not get an appointment when some of the persons lower on the list do. If the appointing officer chooses the second or third eligible, the No. 1 eligible does not get a job at once, but stays on the list until he is appointed or the list is terminated.

X. HOW TO PASS THE INTERVIEW TEST

The examination for which you applied requires an oral interview test. You have already taken the written test and you are now being called for the interview test – the final part of the formal examination.

You may think that it is not possible to prepare for an interview test and that there are no procedures to follow during an interview. Our purpose is to point out some things you can do in advance that will help you and some good rules to follow and pitfalls to avoid while you are being interviewed.

What is an interview supposed to test?

The written examination is designed to test the technical knowledge and competence of the candidate; the oral is designed to evaluate intangible qualities, not readily measured otherwise, and to establish a list showing the relative fitness of each candidate – as measured against his competitors – for the position sought. Scoring is not on the basis of "right" and "wrong," but on a sliding scale of values ranging from "not passable" to "outstanding." As a matter of fact, it is possible to achieve a relatively low score without a single "incorrect" answer because of evident weakness in the qualities being measured.

Occasionally, an examination may consist entirely of an oral test – either an individual or a group oral. In such cases, information is sought concerning the technical knowledges and abilities of the candidate, since there has been no written examination for this purpose. More commonly, however, an oral test is used to supplement a written examination.

Who conducts interviews?

The composition of oral boards varies among different jurisdictions. In nearly all, a representative of the personnel department serves as chairman. One of the members of the board may be a representative of the department in which the candidate would work. In some cases, "outside experts" are used, and, frequently, a businessman or some other representative of the general public is asked to serve. Labor and management or other special groups may be represented. The aim is to secure the services of experts in the appropriate field.

However the board is composed, it is a good idea (and not at all improper or unethical) to ascertain in advance of the interview who the members are and what groups they represent. When you are introduced to them, you will have some idea of their backgrounds and interests, and at least you will not stutter and stammer over their names.

What should be done before the interview?

While knowledge about the board members is useful and takes some of the surprise element out of the interview, there is other preparation which is more substantive. It *is* possible to prepare for an oral interview – in several ways:

1) Keep a copy of your application and review it carefully before the interview

This may be the only document before the oral board, and the starting point of the interview. Know what education and experience you have listed there, and the sequence and dates of all of it. Sometimes the board will ask you to review the highlights of your experience for them; you should not have to hem and haw doing it.

2) Study the class specification and the examination announcement

Usually, the oral board has one or both of these to guide them. The qualities, characteristics or knowledges required by the position sought are stated in these documents. They offer valuable clues as to the nature of the oral interview. For example, if the job involves supervisory responsibilities, the announcement will usually indicate that knowledge of modern supervisory methods and the qualifications of the candidate as a supervisor will be tested. If so, you can expect such questions, frequently in the form of a hypothetical situation which you are expected to solve. NEVER go into an oral without knowledge of the duties and responsibilities of the job you seek.

3) Think through each qualification required

Try to visualize the kind of questions you would ask if you were a board member. How well could you answer them? Try especially to appraise your own knowledge and background in each area, *measured against the job sought*, and identify any areas in which you are weak. Be critical and realistic – do not flatter yourself.

4) Do some general reading in areas in which you feel you may be weak

For example, if the job involves supervision and your past experience has NOT, some general reading in supervisory methods and practices, particularly in the field of human relations, might be useful. Do NOT study agency procedures or detailed manuals. The oral board will be testing your understanding and capacity, not your memory.

5) Get a good night's sleep and watch your general health and mental attitude

You will want a clear head at the interview. Take care of a cold or any other minor ailment, and of course, no hangovers.

What should be done on the day of the interview?

Now comes the day of the interview itself. Give yourself plenty of time to get there. Plan to arrive somewhat ahead of the scheduled time, particularly if your appointment is in the fore part of the day. If a previous candidate fails to appear, the board might be ready for you a bit early. By early afternoon an oral board is almost invariably behind schedule if there are many candidates, and you may have to wait. Take along a book or magazine to read, or your application to review, but leave any extraneous material in the waiting room when you go in for your interview. In any event, relax and compose yourself.

The matter of dress is important. The board is forming impressions about you – from your experience, your manners, your attitude, and your appearance. Give your personal appearance careful attention. Dress your best, but not your flashiest. Choose conservative, appropriate clothing, and be sure it is immaculate. This is a business interview, and your appearance should indicate that you regard it as such. Besides, being well groomed and properly dressed will help boost your confidence.

Sooner or later, someone will call your name and escort you into the interview room. *This is it.* From here on you are on your own. It is too late for any more preparation. But remember, you asked for this opportunity to prove your fitness, and you are here because your request was granted.

What happens when you go in?

The usual sequence of events will be as follows: The clerk (who is often the board stenographer) will introduce you to the chairman of the oral board, who will introduce you to the other members of the board. Acknowledge the introductions before you sit down. Do not be surprised if you find a microphone facing you or a stenotypist sitting by. Oral interviews are usually recorded in the event of an appeal or other review.

Usually the chairman of the board will open the interview by reviewing the highlights of your education and work experience from your application – primarily for the benefit of the other members of the board, as well as to get the material into the record. Do not interrupt or comment unless there is an error or significant misinterpretation; if that is the case, do not hesitate. But do not quibble about insignificant matters. Also, he will usually ask you some question about your education, experience or your present job – partly to get you to start talking and to establish the interviewing "rapport." He may start the actual questioning, or turn it over to one of the other members. Frequently, each member undertakes the questioning on a particular area, one in which he is perhaps most competent, so you can expect each member to participate in the examination. Because time is limited, you may also expect some rather abrupt switches in the direction the questioning takes, so do not be upset by it. Normally, a board member will not pursue a single line of questioning unless he discovers a particular strength or weakness.

After each member has participated, the chairman will usually ask whether any member has any further questions, then will ask you if you have anything you wish to add. Unless you are expecting this question, it may floor you. Worse, it may start you off on an extended, extemporaneous speech. The board is not usually seeking more information. The question is principally to offer you a last opportunity to present further qualifications or to indicate that you have nothing to add. So, if you feel that a significant qualification or characteristic has been overlooked, it is proper to point it out in a sentence or so. Do not compliment the board on the thoroughness of their examination – they have been sketchy, and you know it. If you wish, merely say, "No thank you, I have nothing further to add." This is a point where you can "talk yourself out" of a good impression or fail to present an important bit of information. Remember, *you close the interview yourself*.

The chairman will then say, "That is all, Mr. _____, thank you." Do not be startled; the interview is over, and quicker than you think. Thank him, gather your belongings and take your leave. Save your sigh of relief for the other side of the door.

How to put your best foot forward

Throughout this entire process, you may feel that the board individually and collectively is trying to pierce your defenses, seek out your hidden weaknesses and embarrass and confuse you. Actually, this is not true. They are obliged to make an appraisal of your qualifications for the job you are seeking, and they want to see you in your best light. Remember, they must interview all candidates and a non-cooperative candidate may become a failure in spite of their best efforts to bring out his qualifications. Here are 15 suggestions that will help you:

1) Be natural – Keep your attitude confident, not cocky

If you are not confident that you can do the job, do not expect the board to be. Do not apologize for your weaknesses, try to bring out your strong points. The board is interested in a positive, not negative, presentation. Cockiness will antagonize any board member and make him wonder if you are covering up a weakness by a false show of strength.

2) Get comfortable, but don't lounge or sprawl

Sit erectly but not stiffly. A careless posture may lead the board to conclude that you are careless in other things, or at least that you are not impressed by the importance of the occasion. Either conclusion is natural, even if incorrect. Do not fuss with your clothing, a pencil or an ashtray. Your hands may occasionally be useful to emphasize a point; do not let them become a point of distraction.

3) Do not wisecrack or make small talk

This is a serious situation, and your attitude should show that you consider it as such. Further, the time of the board is limited – they do not want to waste it, and neither should you.

4) Do not exaggerate your experience or abilities

In the first place, from information in the application or other interviews and sources, the board may know more about you than you think. Secondly, you probably will not get away with it. An experienced board is rather adept at spotting such a situation, so do not take the chance.

5) If you know a board member, do not make a point of it, yet do not hide it

Certainly you are not fooling him, and probably not the other members of the board. Do not try to take advantage of your acquaintanceship – it will probably do you little good.

6) Do not dominate the interview

Let the board do that. They will give you the clues – do not assume that you have to do all the talking. Realize that the board has a number of questions to ask you, and do not try to take up all the interview time by showing off your extensive knowledge of the answer to the first one.

7) Be attentive

You only have 20 minutes or so, and you should keep your attention at its sharpest throughout. When a member is addressing a problem or question to you, give him your undivided attention. Address your reply principally to him, but do not exclude the other board members.

8) Do not interrupt

A board member may be stating a problem for you to analyze. He will ask you a question when the time comes. Let him state the problem, and wait for the question.

9) Make sure you understand the question

Do not try to answer until you are sure what the question is. If it is not clear, restate it in your own words or ask the board member to clarify it for you. However, do not haggle about minor elements.

10) Reply promptly but not hastily

A common entry on oral board rating sheets is "candidate responded readily," or "candidate hesitated in replies." Respond as promptly and quickly as you can, but do not jump to a hasty, ill-considered answer.

11) Do not be peremptory in your answers

A brief answer is proper – but do not fire your answer back. That is a losing game from your point of view. The board member can probably ask questions much faster than you can answer them.

12) Do not try to create the answer you think the board member wants

He is interested in what kind of mind you have and how it works – not in playing games. Furthermore, he can usually spot this practice and will actually grade you down on it.

13) Do not switch sides in your reply merely to agree with a board member

Frequently, a member will take a contrary position merely to draw you out and to see if you are willing and able to defend your point of view. Do not start a debate, yet do not surrender a good position. If a position is worth taking, it is worth defending.

14) Do not be afraid to admit an error in judgment if you are shown to be wrong

The board knows that you are forced to reply without any opportunity for careful consideration. Your answer may be demonstrably wrong. If so, admit it and get on with the interview.

15) Do not dwell at length on your present job

The opening question may relate to your present assignment. Answer the question but do not go into an extended discussion. You are being examined for a *new* job, not your present one. As a matter of fact, try to phrase ALL your answers in terms of the job for which you are being examined.

Basis of Rating

Probably you will forget most of these "do's" and "don'ts" when you walk into the oral interview room. Even remembering them all will not ensure you a passing grade. Perhaps you did not have the qualifications in the first place. But remembering them will help you to put your best foot forward, without treading on the toes of the board members.

Rumor and popular opinion to the contrary notwithstanding, an oral board wants you to make the best appearance possible. They know you are under pressure – but they also want to see how you respond to it as a guide to what your reaction would be under the pressures of the job you seek. They will be influenced by the degree of poise you display, the personal traits you show and the manner in which you respond.

ABOUT THIS BOOK

This book contains tests divided into Examination Sections. Go through each test, answering every question in the margin. We have also attached a sample answer sheet at the back of the book that can be removed and used. At the end of each test look at the answer key and check your answers. On the ones you got wrong, look at the right answer choice and learn. Do not fill in the answers first. Do not memorize the questions and answers, but understand the answer and principles involved. On your test, the questions will likely be different from the samples. Questions are changed and new ones added. If you understand these past questions you should have success with any changes that arise. Tests may consist of several types of questions. We have additional books on each subject should more study be advisable or necessary for you. Finally, the more you study, the better prepared you will be. This book is intended to be the last thing you study before you walk into the examination room. Prior study of relevant texts is also recommended. NLC publishes some of these in our Fundamental Series. Knowledge and good sense are important factors in passing your exam. Good luck also helps. So now study this Passbook, absorb the material contained within and take that knowledge into the examination. Then do your best to pass that exam.

EXAMINATION SECTION

EXAMINATION SECTION
TEST 1

DIRECTIONS: Each question or incomplete statement is followed by several suggested answers or completions. Select the one that BEST answers the question or completes the statement. *PRINT THE LETTER OF THE CORRECT ANSWER IN THE SPACE AT THE RIGHT.*

Questions 1-6.

DIRECTIONS: Questions 1 through 6 consist of descriptions of material to which a filing designation must be assigned.

Assume that the matters and cases described in the questions were referred for handling to a government legal office which has its files set up according to these file designations. The file designation consists of a number of characters and punctuation marks as described below.

The first character refers to agencies whose legal work is handled by this office. These agencies are numbered consecutively in the order in which they first submit a matter for attention, and are identified in an alphabetical card index. To date numbers have been assigned to agencies as follows:

Department of Correction	1
Police Department	2
Department of Traffic	3
Department of Consumer Affairs	4
Commission on Human Rights	5
Board of Elections	6
Department of Personnel	7
Board of Estimate	8

The second character is separated from the first character by a dash. The second character is the last digit of the year in which a particular lawsuit or matter is referred to the legal office.

The third character is separated from the second character by a colon and may consist of either of the following:

I. *A sub-number assigned to each lawsuit to which the agency is a party. Lawsuits are numbered consecutively regardless of year. (Lawsuits are brought by or against agency heads rather than agencies themselves, but references are made to agencies for the purpose of simplification.)*

or II. *A capital letter assigned to each matter other than a lawsuit according to subject, the subject being identified in an alphabetical index. To date, letters have been assigned to subjects as follows:*

Citizenship	A	Housing	E
Discrimination	B	Gambling	F
Residence Requirements	C	Freedom of Religion	G
Civil Service Examinations	D		

These referrals are numbered consecutively regardless of year. The first referral by a particular agency on citizenship, for example, would be designated A1, followed by A2, A3, etc.

If no reference is made in a question as to how many letters involving a certain subject or how many lawsuits have been referred by an agency, assume that it is the first.

For each question, choose the file designation which is MOST appropriate for filing the material described in the question.

1. In January 2010, two candidates in a 2009 civil service examination for positions with the Department of Correction filed a suit against the Department of Personnel seeking to set aside an educational requirement for the title.
   The Department of Personnel immediately referred the lawsuit to the legal office for handling.

   A. 1-9:1   B. 1-0:D1   C. 7-9:D1   D. 7-0:1

2. In 2014, the Police Department made its sixth request for an opinion on whether an employee assignment proposed for 2015 could be considered discriminatory.

   A. 2-5:1-B6   B. 2-4:6   C. 2-4:1-B6   D. 2-4:B6

3. In 2015, a lawsuit was brought by the Bay Island Action Committee against the Board of Estimate in which the plaintiff sought withdrawal of approval of housing for the elderly in the Bay Island area given by the Board in 2015.

   A. 8-3:1   B. 8-5:1   C. 8-3:B1   D. 8-5:E1

4. In December 2014, community leaders asked the Police Department to ban outdoor meetings of a religious group on the grounds that the meetings were disrupting the area. Such meetings had been held from time to time during 2014. On January 31, 2015, the Police Department asked the government legal office for an opinion on whether granting this request would violate the worshippers' right to freedom of religion.

   A. 2-4:G-1   B. 2-5:G1   C. 2-5:B-1   D. 2-4:B1

5. In 2014, a woman filed suit against the Board of Elections. She alleged that she had not been permitted to vote at her usual polling place in the 2013 election and had been told she was not registered there. She claimed that she had always voted there and that her record card had been lost. This was the fourth case of its type for this agency.

   A. 6-4:4   B. 6-3:C4   C. 3-4:6   D. 6-3:4

6. A lawsuit was brought in 2011 by the Ace Pinball Machine Company against the Commissioner of Consumer Affairs. The lawsuit contested an ordinance which banned the use of pinball machines on the ground that they are gambling devices.
   This was the third lawsuit to which the Department of Consumer Affairs was a party.

   A. 4-1:1   B. 4-3:F1   C. 4-1:3   D. 3F-4:1

7. You are instructed by your supervisor to type a statement that must be signed by the person making the statement and by three witnesses to the signature. The typed statement will take two pages and will leave no room for signatures if the normal margin is maintained at the bottom of the second page.
In this situation, the PREFERRED method is to type

   A. the signature lines below the normal margin on the second page
   B. nothing further and have the witnesses sign without a typed signature line
   C. the signature lines on a third page
   D. some of the text and the signature lines on a third page

8. Certain legal documents always begin with a statement of venue - that is, the county and state in which the document is executed. This is usually boxed with a parentheses or colons.
The one of the following documents that ALWAYS bears a statement of venue in a prominent position at its head is a(n)

   A. affidavit   B. memorandum of law
   C. contract of sale   D. will

9. A court stenographer is to take stenographic notes and transcribe the statements of a person under oath. The person has a heavy accent and speaks in ungrammatical and broken English.
When he or she is transcribing the testimony, of the following, the BEST thing for them to do is to

   A. transcribe the testimony exactly as spoken, making no grammatical changes
   B. make only the grammatical changes which would clarify the client's statements
   C. make all grammatical changes so that the testimony is in standard English form
   D. ask the client's permission before making any grammatical changes

10. When the material typed on a printed form does not fill the space provided, a Z-ruling is frequently drawn to fill up the unused space.
The MAIN purpose of this practice is to

    A. make the document more pleasing to the eye
    B. indicate that the preceding material is correct
    C. insure that the document is not altered
    D. show that the lawyer has read it

11. After you had typed an original and five copies of a certain document, some changes were made in ink on the original and were initialed by all the parties. The original was signed by all the parties, and the signatures were notarized.
Which of the following should *generally* be typed on the copies BEFORE filing the original and the copies? The inked changes

    A. but not the signatures, initials, or notarial data
    B. the signatures and the initials but not the notarial data
    C. and the notarial data but not the signatures or initials
    D. the signatures, the initials, and the notarial data

12. The first paragraph of a noncourt agreement *generally* contains all of the following EXCEPT the

    A. specific terms of the agreement
    B. date of the agreement
    C. purpose of the agreement
    D. names of the parties involved

13. When typing an answer in a court proceeding, the place where the word ANSWER should be typed on the first page of the document is

    A. at the upper left-hand corner
    B. below the index number and to the right of the box containing the names of the parties to the action
    C. above the index number and to the right of the box containing the names of the parties to the action
    D. to the left of the names of the attorneys for the defendant

14. Which one of the following statements BEST describes the legal document called an acknowledgment?
    It is

    A. an answer to an affidavit
    B. a receipt issued by the court when a document is filed
    C. proof of service of a summons
    D. a declaration that a signature is valid

15. Suppose you typed the original and three copies of a legal document which was dictated by an attorney in your office. He has already signed the original copy, and corrections have been made on all copies.
    Regarding the copies, which one of the following procedures is the PROPER one to follow?

    A. Leave the signature line blank on the copies
    B. Ask the attorney to sign the copies
    C. Print or type the attorney's name on the signature line on the copies
    D. Sign your name to the copies followed by the attorney's initials

16. Suppose your office is defending a particular person in a court action. This person comes to the office and asks to see some of the lawyer's working papers in his file. The lawyer assigned to the case is out of the office at the time.
    You SHOULD

    A. permit him to examine his entire file as long as he does not remove any materials from it
    B. make an appointment for the caller to come back later when the lawyer will be there
    C. ask him what working papers he wants to see and show him only those papers
    D. tell him that he needs written permission from the lawyer in order to see any records

17. Suppose that you receive a phone call from an official who is annoyed about a letter from your office which she just received. The lawyer who dictated the letter is not in the office at the moment.
    Of the following, the BEST action for you to take is to

    A. explain that the lawyer is out but that you will ask the lawyer to return her call when he returns
    B. take down all of the details of her complaint and tell her that you will get back to her with an explanation
    C. refer to the proper file so that you can give her an explanation of the reasons for the letter over the phone
    D. make an appointment for her to stop by the office to speak with the lawyer

18. Suppose that you have taken dictation for an interoffice memorandum. You are asked to prepare it for distribution to four lawyers in your department whose names are given to you. You will type an original and make four copies. Which one of the following is CORRECT with regard to the typing of the lawyers' names?
    The names of all of the lawyers should appear

    A. *only* on the original
    B. on the original and each copy should have the name of one lawyer
    C. on each of the copies but not on the original
    D. on the original and on all of the copies

19. Regarding the correct typing of punctuation, the GENERALLY accepted practice is that there should be

    A. two spaces after a semi-colon
    B. one space before an apostrophe used in the body of a word
    C. no space between parentheses and the matter enclosed
    D. one space before and after a hyphen

20. Suppose you have just completed typing an original and two copies of a letter requesting information. The original is to be signed by a lawyer in your office. The first copy is for the files, and the second is to be used as a reminder to follow up.
    The PROPER time to file the file copy of the letter is

    A. after the letter has been signed and corrections have been made on the copies
    B. before you take the letter to the lawyer for his signature
    C. after a follow-up letter has been sent
    D. after a response to the letter has been received

21. A secretary in a legal office has just typed a letter. She has typed the copy distribution notation on the copies to indicate *blind copy distribution*. This *blind copy* notation shows that

    A. copies of the letter are being sent to persons that the addressee does not know
    B. copies of the letter are being sent to other persons without the addressee's knowledge
    C. a copy of the letter will be enlarged for a legally blind person
    D. a copy of the letter is being given as an extra copy to the addressee

22. Suppose that one of the attorneys in your office dictates material to you without indicating punctuation. He has asked that you give him, as soon as possible, a single copy of a rough draft to be triple-spaced so that he can make corrections.
    Of the following, what is the BEST thing for you to do in this situation?
    A. Assume that no punctuation is desired in the material
    B. Insert the punctuation as you type the rough draft
    C. Transcribe the material exactly as dictated, but attach a note to the attorney stating your suggested changes
    D. Before you start to type the draft, tell the attorney you want to read back your notes so that he can indicate punctuation

23. When it is necessary to type a mailing notation such as CERTIFIED, REGISTERED, or FEDEX on an envelope, the GENERALLY accepted place to type it is
    A. directly above the address
    B. in the area below where the stamp will be affixed
    C. in the lower left-hand corner
    D. in the upper left-hand corner

24. When taking a citation of a case in shorthand, which of the following should you write FIRST if you are having difficulty keeping up with the dictation?
    A. Volume and page number
    B. Title of volume
    C. Name of plaintiff
    D. Name of defendant

25. All of the following abbreviations and their meanings are correctly paired EXCEPT
    A. viz. - namely
    B. ibid. - refer
    C. n.b. - note well
    D. q.v. - which see

KEY (CORRECT ANSWERS)

1. D
2. D
3. B
4. B
5. A

6. C
7. D
8. A
9. A
10. C

11. D
12. A
13. B
14. D
15. C

16. B
17. A
18. D
19. C
20. A

21. B
22. B
23. B
24. A
25. B

EXAMINATION SECTION
TEST 1

DIRECTIONS: Each question or incomplete statement is followed by several suggested answers or completions. Select the one that BEST answers the question or completes the statement. *PRINT THE LETTER OF THE CORRECT ANSWER IN THE SPACE AT THE RIGHT.*

Questions 1-9.

DIRECTIONS: Questions 1 through 9 consist of sentences which may or may not be examples of good English usage. Consider grammar, punctuation, spelling, capitalization, awkwardness, etc. Examine each sentence, and then choose the correct statement about it from the four choices below it. If the English usage in the sentence given is better than it would be with any of the changes suggested in options B, C, and D, choose option A. Do not choose an option that will change the meaning of the sentence.

1. According to Judge Frank, the grocer's sons found guilty of assault and sentenced last Thursday.   1._____

    A. This is an example of acceptable writing.
    B. A comma should be placed after the word *sentenced*.
    C. The word *were* should be placed after *sons*
    D. The apostrophe in *grocer's* should be placed after the *s*.

2. The department heads assistant said that the stenographers should type duplicate copies of all contracts, leases, and bills.   2._____

    A. This is an example of acceptable writing.
    B. A comma should be placed before the word *contracts*.
    C. An apostrophe should be placed before the *s* in *heads*.
    D. Quotation marks should be placed before *the stenographers* and after *bills*.

3. The lawyers questioned the men to determine who was the true property owner?   3._____

    A. This is an example of acceptable writing.
    B. The phrase *questioned the men* should be changed to *asked the men questions*.
    C. The word *was* should be changed to *were*.
    D. The question mark should be changed to a period.

4. The terms stated in the present contract are more specific than those stated in the previous contract.   4._____

    A. This is an example of acceptable writing.
    B. The word *are* should be changed to *is*.
    C. The word *than* should be changed to *then*.
    D. The word *specific* should be changed to *specified*.

5. Of the lawyers considered, the one who argued more skillful was chosen for the job.   5._____

    A. This is an example of acceptable writing.
    B. The word *more* should be replaced by the word *most*.
    C. The word *skillful* should be replaced by the word *skillfully,*
    D. The word *chosen* should be replaced by the word *selected*.

6. Each of the states has a court of appeals; some states have circuit courts.   6.____

   A. This is an example of acceptable writing.
   B. The semi-colon should be changed to a comma.
   C. The word *has* should be changed to *have*.
   D. The word *some* should be capitalized.

7. The court trial has greatly effected the child's mental condition.   7.____

   A. This is an example of acceptable writing.
   B. The word *effected* should be changed to *affected*.
   C. The word *greatly* should be placed after *effected*.
   D. The apostrophe in *child's* should be placed after the *s*.

8. Last week, the petition signed by all the officers was sent to the Better Business Bureau.   8.____

   A. This is an example of acceptable writing.
   B. The phrase *last week* should be placed after *officers*.
   C. A comma should be placed after *petition*.
   D. The word *was* should be changed to *were*.

9. Mr. Farrell claims that he requested form A-12, and three booklets describing court procedures.   9.____

   A. This is an example of acceptable writing.
   B. The word *that* should be eliminated.
   C. A colon should be placed after *requested*.
   D. The comma after *A-12* should be eliminated.

Questions 10-21.

DIRECTIONS: Questions 10 through 21 contain a word in capital letters followed by four suggested meanings of the word. For each question, choose the BEST meaning for the word in capital letters.

10. SIGNATORY - A   10.____

    A. lawyer who draws up a legal document
    B. document that must be signed by a judge
    C. person who signs a document
    D. true copy of a signature

11. RETAINER - A   11.____

    A. fee paid to a lawyer for his services
    B. document held by a third party
    C. court decision to send a prisoner back to custody pending trial
    D. legal requirement to keep certain types of files

12. BEQUEATH - To   12.____

    A. receive assistance from a charitable organization
    B. give personal property by will to another
    C. transfer real property from one person to another
    D. receive an inheritance upon the death of a relative

13. RATIFY - To

    A. approve and sanction
    B. forego
    C. produce evidence
    D. summarize

14. CODICIL - A

    A. document introduced in evidence in a civil action
    B. subsection of a law
    C. type of legal action that can be brought by a plaintiff
    D. supplement or an addition to a will

15. ALIAS

    A. Assumed name
    B. In favor of
    C. Against
    D. A writ

16. PROXY - A(n)

    A. phony document in a real estate transaction
    B. opinion by a judge of a civil court
    C. document containing appointment of an agent
    D. summons in a lawsuit

17. ALLEGED

    A. Innocent
    B. Asserted
    C. Guilty
    D. Called upon

18. EXECUTE - To

    A. complete a legal document by signing it
    B. set requirements
    C. render services to a duly elected executive of a municipality
    D. initiate legal action such as a lawsuit

19. NOTARY PUBLIC - A

    A. lawyer who is running for public office
    B. judge who hears minor cases
    C. public officer, one of whose functions is to administer oaths
    D. lawyer who gives free legal services to persons unable to pay

20. WAIVE - To

    A. disturb a calm state of affairs
    B. knowingly renounce a right or claim
    C. pardon someone for a minor fault
    D. purposely mislead a person during an investigation

21. ARRAIGN - To

    A. prevent an escape
    B. defend a prisoner
    C. verify a document
    D. accuse in a court of law

Questions 22-40.

DIRECTIONS: Questions 22 through 40 each consist of four words which may or may not be spelled correctly. If you find an error in
    only one word, mark your answer A;
    any two words, mark your answer B;
    any three words, mark your answer C;
    none of these words, mark your answer D.

#	1	2	3	4	
22.	occurrence	Febuary	privilege	similiar	22.____
23.	separate	transferring	analyze	column	23.____
24.	develop	license	bankrupcy	abreviate	24.____
25.	subpoena	arguement	dissolution	foreclosure	25.____
26.	exaggerate	fundamental	significance	warrant	26.____
27.	citizen	endorsed	marraige	appraissal	27.____
28.	precedant	univercity	observence	preliminary	28.____
29.	stipulate	negligence	judgment	prominent	29.____
30.	judisial	whereas	release	guardian	30.____
31.	appeal	larcenny	transcrip	jurist	31.____
32.	petition	tenancy	agenda	insurance	32.____
33.	superfical	premise	morgaged	maintainance	33.____
34.	testamony	publically	installment	possessed	34.____
35.	escrow	decree	eviction	miscelaneous	35.____
36.	securitys	abeyance	adhere	corporate	36.____
37.	kaleidoscope	anesthesia	vermilion	tafetta	37.____
38.	congruant	barrenness	plebescite	vigilance	38.____
39.	picnicing	promisory	resevoir	omission	39.____
40.	supersede	banister	wholly	seize	40.____

KEY (CORRECT ANSWERS)

1. C	11. A	21. D	31. B
2. C	12. B	22. B	32. D
3. D	13. A	23. D	33. C
4. A	14. D	24. B	34. B
5. C	15. A	25. A	35. A
6. A	16. C	26. D	36. A
7. B	17. B	27. B	37. A
8. A	18. A	28. C	38. B
9. D	19. C	29. D	39. C
10. C	20. B	30. A	40. D

EXAMINATION SECTION
TEST 1

DIRECTIONS: Each question or incomplete statement is followed by several suggested answers or completions. Select the one that BEST answers the question or completes the statement. *PRINT THE LETTER OF THE CORRECT ANSWER IN THE SPACE AT THE RIGHT.*

Questions 1-25.

DIRECTIONS: In each of Questions 1 through 25, select the lettered word or phrase which means MOST NEARLY the same as the capitalized word.

1. INTERROGATE
    A. question   B. arrest   C. search   D. rebuff

2. PERVERSE
    A. manageable   B. poetic
    C. contrary   D. patient

3. ADVOCATE
    A. champion   B. employ
    C. select   D. advise

4. APPARENT
    A. desirable   B. clear
    C. partial   D. possible

5. INSINUATE
    A. survey   B. strengthen
    C. suggest   D. insist

6. MOMENTOUS
    A. important   B. immediate   C. delayed   D. short

7. AUXILIARY
    A. exciting   B. assisting   C. upsetting   D. available

8. ADMONISH
    A. praise   B. increase   C. warn   D. polish

9. ANTICIPATE
    A. agree   B. expect   C. conceal   D. approve

10. APPREHEND
    A. confuse   B. sentence   C. release   D. seize

11. CLEMENCY
    A. silence   B. freedom   C. mercy   D. severity

12. THWART
    A. enrage   B. strike   C. choke   D. block

13. RELINQUISH
    A. stretch   B. give up   C. weaken   D. flee from
14. CURTAIL
    A. stop   B. reduce   C. repair   D. insult
15. INACCESSIBLE
    A. obstinate   B. unreachable
    C. unreasonable   D. puzzling
16. PERTINENT
    A. related   B. saucy   C. durable   D. impatient
17. INTIMIDATE
    A. encourage   B. hunt   C. beat   D. frighten
18. INTEGRITY
    A. honesty   B. wisdom
    C. understanding   D. persistence
19. UTILIZE
    A. use   B. manufacture
    C. help   D. include
20. SUPPLEMENT
    A. regulate   B. demand   C. add   D. answer
21. INDISPENSABLE
    A. essential   B. neglected
    C. truthful   D. unnecessary
22. ATTAIN
    A. introduce   B. spoil   C. achieve   D. study
23. PRECEDE
    A. break away   B. go ahead
    C. begin   D. come before
24. HAZARD
    A. penalty   B. adventure   C. handicap   D. danger
25. DETRIMENTAL
    A. uncertain   B. harmful   C. fierce   D. horrible

KEY (CORRECT ANSWERS)

1. A	6. A	11. C	16. A	21. A
2. C	7. B	12. D	17. D	22. C
3. A	8. C	13. B	18. A	23. D
4. B	9. B	14. B	19. A	24. D
5. C	10. D	15. B	20. C	25. B

TEST 2

DIRECTIONS: Each question or incomplete statement is followed by several suggested answers or completions. Select the one that BEST answers the question or completes the statement. *PRINT THE LETTER OF THE CORRECT ANSWER IN THE SPACE AT THE RIGHT.*

Questions 1-20.

DIRECTIONS: In each of Questions 1 through 20, select the lettered word or phrase which means MOST NEARLY the same as the capitalized word.

1. IMPLY
   - A. agree to
   - B. hint at
   - C. laugh at
   - D. mimic
   - E. reduce

2. APPRAISAL
   - A. allowance
   - B. composition
   - C. prohibition
   - D. quantity
   - E. valuation

3. DISBURSE
   - A. approve
   - B. expend
   - C. prevent
   - D. relay
   - E. restrict

4. POSTERITY
   - A. back payment
   - B. current procedure
   - C. final effort
   - D. future generations
   - E. rare specimen

5. PUNCTUAL
   - A. clear
   - B. honest
   - C. polite
   - D. prompt
   - E. prudent

6. PRECARIOUS
   - A. abundant
   - B. alarmed
   - C. cautious
   - D. insecure
   - E. placid

7. FOSTER
   - A. delegate
   - B. demote
   - C. encourage
   - D. plead
   - E. surround

8. PINNACLE
   - A. center
   - B. crisis
   - C. outcome
   - D. peak
   - E. personification

9. COMPONENT
   - A. flattery
   - B. opposite
   - C. part
   - D. revision
   - E. trend

10. SOLICIT
    - A. ask
    - B. prohibit
    - C. promise
    - D. revoke
    - E. surprise

11. LIAISON
    A. asset B. coordination C. difference
    D. policy E. procedure

12. ALLEGE
    A. assert B. break C. irritate
    D. reduce E. wait

13. INFILTRATION
    A. consumption B. disposal C. enforcement
    D. penetration E. seizure

14. SALVAGE
    A. announce B. combine C. prolong
    D. save E. try

15. MOTIVE
    A. attack B. favor C. incentive
    D. patience E. tribute

16. PROVOKE
    A. adjust B. incite C. leave
    D. obtain E. practice

17. SURGE
    A. branch B. contract C. revenge
    D. rush E. want

18. MAGNIFY
    A. attract B. demand C. generate
    D. increase E. puzzle

19. PREPONDERANCE
    A. decision B. judgment C. outweighing
    D. submission E. warning

20. ABATE
    A. assist B. coerce C. diminish
    D. indulge E. trade

Questions 21-30.

DIRECTIONS: In each of Questions 21 through 30, select the lettered word or phrase which means MOST NEARLY, the same as, or the opposite of, the capitalized word.

21. VINDICTIVE
    A. centrifugal B. forgiving C. molten
    D. tedious E. vivacious

22. SCOPE
    A. compact B. detriment C. facsimile
    D. potable E. range

23. HINDER
    A. amplify   B. aver   C. method
    D. observe   E. retard

24. IRATE
    A. adhere   B. angry   C. authentic
    D. peremptory   E. vacillate

25. APATHY
    A. accessory   B. availability   C. fervor
    D. pacify   E. stride

26. LUCRATIVE
    A. effective   B. imperfect   C. injurious
    D. timely   E. worthless

27. DIVERSITY
    A. convection   B. slip   C. temerity
    D. uniformity   E. viscosity

28. OVERT
    A. laugh   B. lighter   C. orifice
    D. quay   E. sly

29. SPORADIC
    A. divide   B. incumbrance   C. livid
    D. occasional   E. original

30. PREVARICATE
    A. hesitate   B. increase   C. lie
    D. procrastinate   E. reject

KEY (CORRECT ANSWERS)

1. B	11. B	21. B
2. E	12. A	22. E
3. B	13. D	23. E
4. D	14. D	24. B
5. D	15. C	25. C
6. D	16. B	26. E
7. C	17. D	27. D
8. D	18. D	28. E
9. C	19. C	29. D
10. A	20. C	30. C

TEST 3

DIRECTIONS: Each question or incomplete statement is followed by several suggested answers or completions. Select the one that BEST answers the question or completes the statement. *PRINT THE LETTER OF THE CORRECT ANSWER IN THE SPACE AT THE RIGHT.*

Questions 1-30.

DIRECTIONS: In each of Questions 1 through 30, select the lettered word which means MOST NEARLY the same as the capitalized word.

1. AVARICE
   A. flight   B. greed   C. pride   D. thrift

2. PREDATORY
   A. offensive   B. plundering
   C. previous   D. timeless

3. VINDICATE
   A. clear   B. conquer   C. correct   D. illustrate

4. INVETERATE
   A. backward   B. erect   C. habitual   D. lucky

5. DISCERN
   A. describe   B. fabricate   C. recognize   D. seek

6. COMPLACENT
   A. indulgent   B. listless   C. overjoyed   D. satisfied

7. ILLICIT
   A. insecure   B. unclear   C. unlawful   D. unlimited

8. PROCRASTINATE
   A. declare   B. multiply   C. postpone   D. steal

9. IMPASSIVE
   A. calm   B. frustrated
   C. thoughtful   D. unhappy

10. AMICABLE
    A. cheerful   B. flexible
    C. friendly   D. poised

11. FEASIBLE
    A. breakable   B. easy
    C. likeable   D. practicable

12. INNOCUOUS
    A. harmless   B. insecure
    C. insincere   D. unfavorable

13. OSTENSIBLE
    A. apparent   B. hesitant   C. reluctant   D. showy

14. INDOMITABLE
    A. excessive   B. unconquerable
    C. unreasonable   D. unthinkable

15. CRAVEN
    A. cowardly   B. hidden   C. miserly   D. needed

16. ALLAY
    A. discuss   B. quiet   C. refine   D. remove

17. ALLUDE
    A. denounce   B. refer   C. state   D. support

18. NEGLIGENCE
    A. carelessness   B. denial
    C. objection   D. refusal

19. AMEND
    A. correct   B. destroy   C. end   D. list

20. RELEVANT
    A. conclusive   B. careful
    C. obvious   D. related

21. VERIFY
    A. challenge   B. change   C. confirm   D. reveal

22. INSIGNIFICANT
    A. incorrect   B. limited
    C. unimportant   D. undesirable

23. RESCIND
    A. annul   B. deride   C. extol   D. indulge

24. AUGMENT
    A. alter   B. increase   C. obey   D. perceive

25. AUTONOMOUS
    A. conceptual   B. constant
    C. defamatory   D. independent

26. TRANSCRIPT
    A. copy   B. report   C. sentence   D. termination

27. DISCORDANT
    A. quarrelsome   B. comprised
    C. effusive   D. harmonious

28. DISTEND
    A. constrict   B. dilate   C. redeem   D. silence

29. EMANATE
    A. bridge   B. coherency   C. conquer   D. flow

30. EXULTANT
    A. easily upset
    B. in high spirits
    C. subject to moods
    D. very much over-priced

KEY (CORRECT ANSWERS)

1. B	11. D	21. C
2. B	12. A	22. C
3. A	13. A	23. A
4. C	14. B	24. B
5. C	15. A	25. D
6. D	16. B	26. A
7. C	17. B	27. A
8. C	18. A	28. B
9. A	19. A	29. D
10. C	20. D	30. B

EXAMINATION SECTION
TEST 1

DIRECTIONS: Each question or incomplete statement is followed by several suggested answers or completions. Select the one that BEST answers the question or completes the statement. *PRINT THE LETTER OF THE CORRECT ANSWER IN THE SPACE AT THE RIGHT.*

1. The ∧ or caret symbol is a proofreader's mark which means that a
   A. space should have been left between two words
   B. new paragraph should be indicated
   C. word, phrase, or punctuation mark should be inserted
   D. word that is abbreviated should be spelled out

2. Of the following items, the one which should NOT be omitted from a typed inter-office memorandum is the
   A. salutation
   B. complementary closing
   C. formal signature
   D. names of those to receive copies

3. A typed rough draft should be double-spaced and should have wide margins PRIMARILY in order to
   A. save time in making typing corrections
   B. provide room for making insertions and corrections
   C. insure that the report is well-organized
   D. permit faster typing of the draft

4. In tabular reports, when a main heading, secondary heading, and single line of columnar headings are used, a triple space (2 blank lines) would be used after the _____ heading(s).
   A. main
   B. secondary
   C. columnar
   D. main and secondary

5. You have been requested to type a letter to Mr. Brown, a district attorney of a small town.
   Of the following, the CORRECT salutation to use is Dear
   A. District Attorney Brown:
   B. Mr. District Attorney:
   C. Mr. Brown:
   D. Honorable Brown:

6. A form letter that is sent to the public can be made to look more personal in appearance by doing all of the following EXCEPT
   A. using a meter stamp on the envelope of the letter
   B. having the letter signed with pen and ink
   C. using a good quality of paper for the letter
   D. matching the type used in the letter with that used for fill-ins

7. A senior typist opens a word-processing application to instruct a typist to create a table that contains three column headings. Under each column heading are three items.
Of the following, which sequence should the senior typist tell the typist to use when creating this table?
    A. First type the headings, and then type the items under them, a column at a time
    B. type each heading with its column of items under it, one column at a time
    C. first type the column of items, then center the headings above them
    D. type the headings and items across the page line by line

7.____

8. When a letter is addressed to an agency and a particular person should see it, an *attention line* is used.
This attention line is USUALLY found
    A. on the envelope only
    B. above the address
    C. below the address
    D. after the agency named in the address

8.____

9. The typing technique of *justifying* is used to
    A. decide how wide margins of different sized letters should be
    B. make all the lines of copy end evenly on the right-hand margin
    C. center headings above columns on tabular typed material
    D. condense the amount of space that is needed to make a manuscript look presentable

9.____

10. The date line on a letter is typed correctly when the date is ALL on one line
    A. with the month written out   B. with slashes between the numbers
    C. and the month is abbreviated   D. with a period at the end

10.____

11. When considering how wide to make a column when typing a table, the BASIC rule to follow is that the column should be as wide as the longest
    A. item in the body of the column
    B. heading of all of the columns
    C. item in the body or heading of that column
    D. heading or the longest item in the body of any column on that page

11.____

12. When a lengthy quotation is included in a letter or a report, it must be indicated that it is quoted material. This may be done by
    A. enclosing the quotation in parentheses
    B. placing an exclamation point at the end of the quotation
    C. using the apostrophe marks
    D. indenting from the regular margins on the left and right

12.____

13. In order to reach the highest rate of speed and the greatest degree of accuracy while typing, it is LEAST important to
    A. maintain good posture
    B. keep the hands and arms at a comfortable level
    C. strike the keys evenly
    D. keep the typing action in the wrists

14. It has been shown that the rate of typing and dictation drops when the secretary is not familiar with the language or topic of the copy.
    A practice that a supervisor might BEST advise to improve the knowledge and therefore increase the rate of typing dictation for such material would be for the secretary to
    A. plan a conference with her supervisor to discuss the subject matter
    B. read and review correspondence and related technical journals that come into the office
    C. recopy or retype previously transcribed material as practice
    D. withdraw sample materials from the files to take home for study

15. The one of the following in which the tab key is NOT generally used is the
    A. placement of the complimentary close and signature line
    B. indentation of paragraphs
    C. placement of the date line
    D. centering of title headings

16. In order for a business letter to be effective, it is LEAST important that it
    A. say what is meant simply and directly
    B. be written in formal language
    C. include all information the receiver needs to know
    D. be courteously written

17. If you are momentarily called away from your desk while typing a report of a confidential nature, you should cover or turn the copy over and
    A. remove the page being typed from the computer and file the report
    B. ask someone to watch your desk for you
    C. close the document so that the page is not visible
    D. spread a folder over the computer screen to conceal it

18. When typing a table that contains a column of figures and a column of words, the PROPER alignment of the column of figures and the column of words should be an even _____ the column of words.
    A. right-hand edge for the column of numbers and an even left-hand edge for
    B. right-hand edge for both the column of numbers and
    C. left-hand edge for the column of numbers and an even right-hand edge for
    D. left-hand edge for both the column of numbers and

19. The word *re*, when used in a memorandum, refers to the information that is on the _____ line. 19.____
    A. identification   B. subject   C. attention   D. reference

20. Of the following uses of the period, the one which requires NO spacing after it when it is typed is when the period 20.____
    A. follows an abbreviation or an initial
    B. follows a figure or letter at the beginning of a line in a list of items
    C. comes between the initials that make up a single abbreviation
    D. comes at the end of a sentence

21. This <u>mark</u> is a proofreader's mark meaning the word 21.____
    A. is misspelled
    B. should be underlined
    C. should be bold
    D. should be capitalized

22. When typing a report that is double-spaced, the STANDARD recommended practice for indicating the start of new paragraphs is to 22.____
    A. double-space between paragraphs and indent the first word at least five spaces
    B. triple-space between paragraphs and indent the first word at least five spaces
    C. triple-space between paragraphs and type block style at the margin
    D. double-space between paragraphs and type block style at the margin

23. In order to center a heading on a sheet of paper once the center of the paper has been found, the EASIEST and MOST efficient method to use is 23.____
    A. note the scale at each end of the heading to be centered and divide by two
    B. backspace from the center of the paper one space for every two letters and spaces in the heading
    C. arrange the heading around the middle number on the computer
    D. use a ruler to mark off the amount of space from both sides of the center of the paper that should be taken up by the heading

24. You are about to type a single-spaced letter from a typewritten draft. In order to center this letter from top to bottom, your FIRST step should be to 24.____
    A. determine the number of spaces needed for the top and bottom margins
    B. determine the number of spaces needed for the left and right margins
    C. count the number of lines, including blank ones, which will be used for the letter
    D. subtract from the number of writing lines on the sheet of paper the number of lines that will not be used for the letter

25. When typing a table which lists several amounts of money and the total in a column, the dollar sign should be placed in front of the 25.____
    A. first dollar amount only
    B. total dollar amount only
    C. first and total dollar amounts only
    D. all of the amounts of money in the column

26. If a legal document is being prepared and requires necessary information to be typed into blank areas on preprinted legal forms, the margins for a line of typewritten material should be determined PRIMARILY by
    A. counting the total number of words to be typed
    B. the margins set for the pre-printed matter
    C. spacing backwards from the right margin rule
    D. the estimated width and height of the material to be entered

26.____

27. When checking for errors in material you've typed, it is BEST to
    A. proofread the material and use the spell-check function in combination
    B. give the material to someone else to review
    C. run the spell-check function and auto-correct all found errors
    D. proofread the material then e-mail it to another typist for final approval

27.____

28. Assume that Mr. Frank Foran is an acting official. In a letter written to him, the word *acting* would
    A. be used with the title in the address and in the salutation
    B. not be used with the title in the address
    C. be used with the title in the address but not in the salutation
    D. not be used with the title in the address or in the salutation

28.____

29. The software program that requires proficiency in typing in order to best utilize its MOST important features is
    A. Microsoft Excel   B. Adobe Reader
    C. Microsoft Word   D. Intuit QuickBooks

29.____

30. The MAIN reason for keeping a careful record of incoming mail is that
    A. greater speed and accuracy is obtained for answering outgoing mail
    B. this record is legal evidence
    C. it develops the efficiency of the office clerks
    D. the information may be useful some day

30.____

KEY (CORRECT ANSWERS)

1.	C	11.	C	21.	D
2.	D	12.	D	22.	A
3.	B	13.	D	23.	B
4.	B	14.	B	24.	C
5.	C	15.	D	25.	C
6.	A	16.	B	26.	B
7.	D	17.	C	27.	A
8.	C	18.	A	28.	C
9.	B	19.	B	29.	C
10.	A	20.	C	30.	A

TEST 2

DIRECTIONS: Each question or incomplete statement is followed by several suggested answers or completions. Select the one that BEST answers the question or completes the statement. *PRINT THE LETTER OF THE CORRECT ANSWER IN THE SPACE AT THE RIGHT.*

Questions 1-4.

DIRECTIONS: Questions 1 through 4 are to be answered SOLELY on the basis of the information contained in the following passage which is taken from a typing test.

Modern office methods, geared to ever higher speeds and aimed at ever greater efficiency, are largely the result of the typewriter. The typewriter is a substitute for handwriting; and, in the hands of a skilled typist, not only turns out letters and other documents at least three times faster than a penman can do the work, but turns out the greater volume more uniformly and legibly. With the use of carbon paper and onionskin paper, identical copies can be made at the same time.

The typewriter, besides its effect on the conduct of business and government, has had a very important effect on the position of women. The typewriter has done much to bring women into business and government, and today there are vastly more women than men typists. Many women have used the keys of the typewriter to climb the ladder to responsible managerial positions.

The typewriter, as its name implies, employs type to make an ink impression on paper. For many years, the manual typewriter was the standard machine used. Today, the electric typewriter is dominant, with electronic typewriters, word processors, and computers coming into wider use.

The mechanism of the office manual typewriter includes a set of keys arranged systematically in rows; a semicircular frame of type, connected to the keys by levers; the carriage or paper carrier; a rubber roller called a platen, against which the type strikes; and an inked ribbon which makes the impression of the type character when the key strikes it. This machine, once omnipresent, is an antique today.

1. The above passage mentions a number of good features of the combination of a skilled typist and a typewriter.
   Of the following, the feature which is NOT mentioned in the passage is
   A. speed B. uniformity C. reliability D. legibility

   1._____

2. According to the above passage, a skilled typist can
   A. turn out at least five carbon copies of typed matter
   B. type at least three times faster than a penman can write
   C. type more than 80 words a minute
   D. readily move into a managerial position

   2._____

3. According to the above passage, which of the following is NOT part of the mechanism of a manual typewriter?
   A. Carbon paper
   B. Paper carrier
   C. Platen
   D. Inked ribbon

4. According to the above passage, the typewriter has helped
   A. men more than women in business
   B. women in career advancement into management
   C. men and women equally, but women have taken better advantage of it
   D. more women than men, because men generally dislike routine typing work

5. Standard rules for typing spacing have developed through usage. According to these rules, two spaces are left after a(n)
   A. colon
   B. comma
   C. hyphen
   D. opening parenthesis

6. Assume that you have to type the heading CENTERING TYPED HEADINGS on a piece of paper which extends from 0 to 100 on the typewriter scale. You want the heading to be perfectly centered on the paper.
   In order to find the proper point on the typewriter scale at which to begin typing, you should determine the paper's center point on the typewriter scale and then _____ the number of letters and spaces in the heading.
   A. add
   B. add one-half
   C. subtract
   D. subtract one-half

7. While typing from a rough draft, the practice of reading a line ahead of what you are now typing is considered to be a
   A. *good* practice; it may prepare your fingers for the words which you will be typing
   B. *good* practice; it may help you to review the subject matter contained in the material
   C. *poor* practice; it may increase your typing speed so that your accuracy is decreased
   D. *poor* practice; it may cause you to lose your concentration and make errors in the words you are presently typing

8. Assume that you are transcribing a letter and you are not sure how to divide a word at the end of a line you are typing.
   The BEST way to determine where to divide the word is by
   A. asking your supervisor
   B. asking the person who dictated the letter
   C. checking with other stenographers
   D. looking up the word in a dictionary

9. When taking proper care of a typewriter, it is NOT a desirable action to
   A. clean the feed rolls with a cloth
   B. dust the exterior surface of the machine
   C. oil the rubber parts of the machine
   D. use a type-cleaning brush to clean the keys

10. Of the following, the LEAST desirable action to take when typing a rough draft of a report is to
    A. cross out typing errors instead of erasing them
    B. double or triple space between lines
    C. provide large margins on all sides of the typing paper
    D. use letterhead or onionskin paper

11. The date line of every business letter should indicate the month, the day of the month, and the year.
    The MOST common practice when typing a date line is to type it as
    A. Jan. 12, 2018   B. January 12, 2018
    C. 1-12-18   D. 1/12/18

Questions 12-16.

DIRECTIONS: Questions 12 through 16 are to be answered SOLELY on the basis of the information provided in the following passage.

A written report is a communication of information from one person to another. It is an account of some matter especially investigated, however routine that matter may be. The ultimate basis of any good written report is facts, which became known through observation and verification. Good written reports may seem to be no more than general ideas and opinions. However, in such cases, the facts leading to these opinions were gathered, verified, and reported earlier, and the opinions are dependent upon these facts. Good style, proper form, and emphasis cannot make a good written report out of unreliable information and bad judgments but on the other hand, solid investigation and brilliant thinking are not likely to become very useful until they are effectively communicated to others. If a person's work calls for written reports, then his work is often no better than his written reports.

12. Based on the information in the above passage, it can be concluded that opinions expressed in a report should be
    A. based on facts which are gathered and reported
    B. emphasized repeatedly when they result from a special investigation
    C. kept to a minimum
    D. separated from the body of the report

13. In the above passage, the one of the following which is mentioned as a way of establishing facts is
    A. authority   B. communication
    C. reporting   D. verification

14. According to the above passage, the characteristic shared by ALL written reports is that they are
    A. accounts of routine matters
    B. transmissions of information
    C. reliable and logical
    D. written in proper form

15. Which of the following conclusions can LOGICALLY be drawn from the information given in the above passage?
    A. Brilliant thinking can make up for unreliable information in a report.
    B. One method of judging an individual's work is the quality of the written reports he is required to submit.
    C. Proper form and emphasis can make a good report out of unreliable information.
    D. Good written reports that seem to be no more than general ideas should be rewritten.

16. Which of the following suggested titles would be MOST appropriate for this passage?
    A. GATHERING AND ORGANIZING FACTS
    B. TECHNIQUES OF OBSERVATION
    C. NATURE AND PURPOSE OF REPORTS
    D. REPORTS AND OPINIONS: DIFFERENCES AND SIMILARITIES

Questions 17-25

DIRECTIONS: Each of Questions 17 through 25 consists of a sentence which may or may not be an example of good English usage. Examine each sentence, considering grammar, punctuation, spelling, capitalization, and awkwardness. Then choose the correct statement about it from the four choices below it. If the English usage in the sentence given is better than any of the changes suggested in Choices B, C, or D, pick choice A. Do NOT pick a choice that will change the meaning of the sentence.

17. We attended a staff conference on Wednesday the new safety and fire rules were discussed.
    A. This is an example of acceptable writing.
    B. The words *safety*, *fire*, and *rules* should begin with capital letters.
    C. There should be a comma after the word *Wednesday*.
    D. There should be a period after the word *Wednesday*, and the word *the* should begin with a capital letter.

18. Neither the dictionary or the telephone directory could be found in the office library.
    A. This is an example of acceptable writing.
    B. The word *or* should be changed to *nor*.
    C. The word *library* should be spelled *libery*.
    D. The word *neither* should be changed to *either*.

19. The report would have been typed correctly if the typist cold read the draft.   19.____
    A. This is an example of acceptable writing.
    B. The word *would* should be removed.
    C. The word *have* should be inserted after the word *could*.
    D. The word *correctly* should be changed to *correct*.

20. The supervisor brought the reports and forms to an employees desk.   20.____
    A. This is an example of acceptable writing.
    B. The word *brought* should be changed to *took*.
    C. There should be a comma after the word *reports* and a comma after the word *forms*.
    D. The word *employees* should be spelled *employee's*.

21. It's important for all the office personnel to submit their vacation schedules on time.   21.____
    A. This is an example of acceptable writing.
    B. The word *It's* should be spelled *Its*.
    C. The word *their* should be spelled *they're*.
    D. The word *personnel* should be spelled *personal*.

22. The supervisor wants that all staff members report to the office at 9:00 A.M.   22.____
    A. This is an example of acceptable writing.
    B. The word *that* should be removed and the word *to* should be inserted after the word *members*.
    C. There should be a comma after the word *wants* and a comma after the word *office*.
    D. The word *wants* should be changed to *want* and the word *shall* should be inserted after the word *members*.

23. Every morning the clerk opens the office mail and distributes it.   23.____
    A. This is an example of acceptable writing.
    B. The word *opens* should be changed to *open*.
    C. The word *mail* should be changed to *letters*.
    D. The word *it* should be changed to *them*.

24. The secretary typed more fast on an electric typewriter than on a manual typewriter.   24.____
    A. This is an example of acceptable writing.
    B. The words *more fast* should be changed to *faster*.
    C. There should be a comma after the words *electric typewriter*.
    D. The word *than* should be changed to *then*.

25. The new stenographer needed a desk a typewriter, a chair and a blotter.   25.____
    A. This is an example of acceptable writing.
    B. The word *blotter* should be spelled *blodder*.
    C. The word *stenographer* should begin with a capital letter.
    D. There should be a comma after the word *desk*.

KEY (CORRECT ANSWERS)

1.	C	11.	B
2.	B	12	A
3.	A	13.	D
4.	B	14.	B
5.	A	15.	B
6.	D	16.	C
7.	D	17.	D
8.	D	18.	B
9.	C	19.	C
10.	D	20.	D

21. A
22. B
23. A
24. B
25. D

EXAMINATION SECTION
TEST 1

DIRECTIONS: Each question or incomplete statement is followed by several suggested answers or completions. Select the one that BEST answers the question or completes the statement. *PRINT THE LETTER OF THE CORRECT ANSWER IN THE SPACE AT THE RIGHT.*

1. A coworker has e-mailed a file containing a spreadsheet for your review. Which of the following programs will open the file?

    A. Adobe Reader
    B. Microsoft Excel
    C. Microsoft PowerPoint
    D. Adobe Illustrator

2. A report needs to be forwarded immediately to a supervisor in another office. Which of the following is the LEAST effective way of giving the supervisor the report?

    A. scanning the report and e-mailing the file
    B. faxing it to the supervisor's office
    C. uploading it to the office network and informing the supervisor
    D. waiting for the supervisor to come to your office and giving it to him/her then

3. Suppose your supervisor is on the telephone in his office and an applicant arrives for a scheduled interview with him.
Of the following, the BEST procedure to follow ordinarily is to

    A. informally chat with the applicant in your office until your supervisor has finished his phone conversation
    B. escort him directly into your supervisor's office and have him wait for him there
    C. inform your supervisor of the applicant's arrival and try to make the applicant feel comfortable while waiting
    D. have him hang up his coat and tell him to go directly in to see your supervisor

Questions 4-9.

DIRECTIONS: Questions 4 through 9 each consist of a sentence which may or may not be an example of good English usage. Consider grammar, punctuation, spelling, capitalization, awkwardness, etc. Examine each sentence, and then choose the correct statement about it from the four choices below it. If the English usage in the sentence given is better than any of the changes suggested in options B, C, or D, choose option A. Do not choose an option that will change the meaning of the sentence.

4. The report, along with the accompanying documents, were submitted for review.

    A. This is an example of acceptable writing.
    B. The words *were submitted* should be changed to *was submitted*.
    C. The word *accompanying* should be spelled *accompaning*.
    D. The comma after the word *report* should be taken out.

5. If others must use your files, be certain that they understand how the system works, but insist that you do all the filing and refiling.   5.____
   A. This is an example of acceptable writing.
   B. There should be a period after the word *works*, and the word *but* should start a new sentence.
   C. The words *filing* and *refiling* should be spelled *fileing* and *refileing*.
   D. There should be a comma after the word *but*.

6. The appeal was not considered because of its late arrival.   6.____
   A. This is an example of acceptable writing.
   B. The word *its* should be changed to *it's*.
   C. The word *its* should be changed to *the*.
   D. The words *late arrival* should be changed to *arrival late*.

7. The letter must be read carefuly to determine under which subject it should be filed.   7.____
   A. This is an example of acceptable writing.
   B. The word *under* should be changed to *at*.
   C. The word *determine* should be spelled *determin*.
   D. The word *carefuly* should be spelled *carefully*.

8. He showed potential as an office manager, but he lacked skill in delegating work.   8.____
   A. This is an example of acceptable writing.
   B. The word *delegating* should be spelled *delagating*.
   C. The word *potential* should be spelled *potencial*.
   D. The words *lie lacked* should be changed to *was lacking*.

9. His supervisor told him that it would be all right to receive personal mail at the office.   9.____
   A. This is an example of acceptable writing.
   B. The words *all right* should be changed to *alright*.
   C. The word *personal* should be spelled *personel*.
   D. The word *mail* should be changed to *letters*.

Questions 10-13.

DIRECTIONS: Questions 10 through 13 are to be answered SOLELY on the basis of the information given in the following passage.

Typed pages can reflect the simplicity of modern art in a machine age. Lightness and evenness can be achieved by proper layout and balance of typed lines and white space. Instead of solid, cramped masses of uneven, crowded typing, there should be a pleasing balance up and down as well as horizontal.

To have real balance, your page must have a center. The eyes see the center of the sheet slightly above the real center. This is the way both you and the reader see it. Try imagining a line down the center of the page that divides the paper in equal halves. On either side of your paper, white space and blocks of typing need to be similar in size and shape. Although left and right margins should be equal, top and bottom margins need not be as exact. It looks better to hold a bottom border wider than a top margin, so that your typing rests *upon a cushion of white space. To add interest to the appearance of the page, try making one paragraph between one-half and two-thirds the size of an adjacent paragraph.*

Thus, by taking full advantage of your typewriter, the pages that you type will not only be accurate but will also be attractive.

10. It can be inferred from the passage that the BASIC importance of proper balancing on a typed page is that proper balancing

    A. makes a typed page a work of modern art
    B. provides exercise in proper positioning of a typewriter
    C. increases the amount of typed copy on the paper
    D. draws greater attention and interest to the page

11. A reader will tend to see the center of a typed page

    A. somewhat higher than the true center
    B. somewhat lower than the true center
    C. on either side of the true center
    D. about two-thirds of an inch above the true center

12. Which of the following suggestions is NOT given by the passage?

    A. Bottom margins may be wider than top borders.
    B. Keep all paragraphs approximately the same size.
    C. Divide your page with an imaginary line down the middle.
    D. Side margins should be equalized.

13. Of the following, the BEST title for this passage is:

    A. INCREASING THE ACCURACY OF THE TYPED PAGE
    B. DETERMINATION OF MARGINS FOR TYPED COPY
    C. LAYOUT AND BALANCE OF THE TYPED PAGE
    D. HOW TO TAKE FULL ADVANTAGE OF THE TYPEWRITER

14. In order to type addresses on a large number of envelopes MOST efficiently, you should

    A. insert another envelope into the typewriter before removing each typed envelope
    B. take each typed envelope out of the machine before starting the next envelope
    C. insert several envelopes into the machine at one time, keeping all top and bottom edges even
    D. insert several envelopes into the machine at one time, keeping the top edge of each envelope two inches below the top edge of the one beneath it

15. A senior typist has completed copying a statistical report from a rough draft.
    Of the following, the BEST way to be sure that her typing is correct is for the typist to

    A. fold the rough draft, line it up with the typed copy, compare one-half of the columns with the original, and have a co-worker compare the other half
    B. check each line of the report as it is typed and then have a co-worker check each line again after the entire report is finished

C. have a co-worker add each column and check the totals on the typed copy with the totals on the original
D. have a co-worker read aloud from the rough draft while the typist checks the typed copy and then have the typist read while the co-worker checks

16. In order to center a heading when typing a report, you should

    A. measure your typing paper with a ruler and begin the heading one-third of the way in from the left margin
    B. begin the heading at the point on the typewriter scale which is 50 minus the number of letters in the heading
    C. multiply the number of characters in the heading by two and begin the heading that number of spaces in from the left margin
    D. begin the heading at the point on the scale which is equal to the center point of your paper minus one-half the number of characters and spaces in the heading

17. Which of the following recommendations concerning the use of copy paper for making typewritten copies should NOT be followed?

    A. Copy papers should be checked for wrinkles before being used.
    B. Legal-size copy paper may be folded if it is too large to fit into a convenient drawer space.
    C. When several sheets of paper are being used, they should be fastened with a paper clip at the top after insertion in the typewriter.
    D. For making many copies, paper of the same weight and brightness should be used.

18. Assume that a new typist, Norma Garcia, has been assigned to work under your supervision and is reporting to work for the first time. You formally introduce Norma to her co-workers and suggest that a few of the other typists explain the office procedures and typing formats to her. The practice of instructing Norma in her duties in this manner is

    A. *good* because she will be made to feel at home
    B. *good* because she will learn more about routine office tasks from co-workers than from you
    C. *poor* because her co-workers will resent the extra work
    D. *poor* because you will not have enough control over her training

19. Suppose that Jean Brown, a typist, is typing a letter following the same format that she has always used. However, she notices that the other two typists in her office are also typing letters, but are using a different format. Jean is concerned that she might not have been informed of a change in format.
    Of the following, the FIRST action that Jean should take is to

    A. seek advice from her supervisor as to which format to use
    B. ask the other typists whether she should use a new format for typing letters
    C. disregard the format that the other typists are using and continue to type in the format she had been using
    D. use the format that the other typists are using, assuming that it is a newly accepted method

20. Suppose that the new office to which you have been assigned has put up Christmas decorations, and a Christmas party is being planned by the city agency in which you work. However, nothing has been said about Christmas gifts.
It would be CORRECT for you to assume that

    A. you are expected to give a gift to your supervisor
    B. your supervisor will give you a gift
    C. you are expected to give gifts only to your subordinates
    D. you will neither receive gifts nor will you be expected to give any

KEY (CORRECT ANSWERS)

1.	B	11.	A
2.	D	12.	B
3.	C	13.	C
4.	B	14.	A
5.	A	15.	D
6.	A	16.	D
7.	D	17.	B
8.	A	18.	D
9.	A	19.	A
10.	D	20.	D

TEST 2

DIRECTIONS: Each question or incomplete statement is followed by several suggested answers or completions. Select the one that BEST answers the question or completes the statement. *PRINT THE LETTER OF THE CORRECT ANSWER IN THE SPACE AT THE RIGHT.*

1. The supervisor you assist is under great pressure to meet certain target dates. He has scheduled an emergency meeting to take place in a few days, and he asks you to send out notices immediately. As you begin to prepare the notices, however, you realize he has scheduled the meeting for a Saturday, which is not a working day. Also, you sense that your supervisor is not in a good mood.
   Which of the following is the MOST effective method of handling this situation?

   A. Change the meeting date to the first working day after that Saturday and send out the notices.
   B. Change the meeting date to a working day on which his calendar is clear and send out the notices.
   C. Point out to your supervisor that the date is a Saturday.
   D. Send out the notices as they are since you have received specific instructions.

1.____

Questions 2-7.

DIRECTIONS: Questions 2 through 7 each consist of a sentence which may or may not be an example of good English usage. Consider grammar, punctuation, spelling, capitalization, awkwardness, etc. Examine each sentence, and then choose the correct statement about it from the four choices below it. If the English usage in the sentence given is better than any of the changes suggested in options B, C, or D, choose option A. Do not choose an option that will change the meaning of the sentence.

2. The typist used an extention cord in order to connect her typewriter to the outlet nearest to her desk.

   A. This is an example of acceptable writing.
   B. A period should be placed after the word *cord,* and the word *in* should have a capital I.
   C. A comma should be placed after the word *typewriter.*
   D. The word *extention* should be spelled *extension.*

2.____

3. He would have went to the conference if he had received an invitation.

   A. This is an example of acceptable writing.
   B. The word *went* should be replaced by the word *gone.*
   C. The word *had* should be replaced by *would have.*
   D. The word *conference* should be spelled *conferance.*

3.____

4. In order to make the report neater, he spent many hours rewriting it.

   A. This is an example of acceptable writing.
   B. The word *more* should be inserted before the word *neater.*
   C. There should be a colon after the word *neater.*
   D. The word *spent* should be changed to *have spent.*

4.____

5. His supervisor told him that he should of read the memorandum more carefully. 5.____
   A. This is an example of acceptable writing.
   B. The word *memorandum* should be spelled *memorandom*.
   C. The word *of* should be replaced by the word *have*.
   D. The word *carefully* should be replaced by the word *careful*.

6. It was decided that two separate reports should be written. 6.____
   A. This is an example of acceptable writing.
   B. A comma should be inserted after the word *decided*.
   C. The word *be* should be replaced by the word *been*.
   D. A colon should be inserted after the word *that*.

7. She don't seem to understand that the work must be done as soon as possible. 7.____
   A. This is an example of acceptable writing.
   B. The word *doesn't* should replace the word *don't*.
   C. The word *why* should replace the word *that*.
   D. The word *as* before the word *soon* should be eliminated.

Questions 8-11.

DIRECTIONS: Questions 8 through 11 are to be answered SOLELY on the basis of the following passage.

There is nothing that will take the place of good sense on the part of the stenographer. You may be perfect in transcribing exactly what the dictator says and your speed may be adequate; but without an understanding of the dictator's intent as well as his words, you are likely to be a mediocre secretary.

A serious error that is made when taking dictation is putting down something that does not make sense. Most people who dictate material would rather be asked to repeat and explain than to receive transcribed material which has errors due to inattention or doubt. Many dictators request that their grammar be corrected by their secretaries; but unless specifically asked to do so, secretaries should not do it without first checking with the dictator. Secretaries should be aware that, in some cases, dictators may use incorrect grammar or slang expressions to create a particular effect.

Some people dictate commas, periods, and paragraphs, while others expect the stenographer to know when, where, and how to punctuate. A well-trained secretary should be able to indicate the proper punctuation by listening to the pauses and tones of the dictator's voice.

A stenographer who has taken dictation from the same person for a period of time should be able to understand him under most conditions. By increasing her tact, alertness, and efficiency, a secretary can become more competent.

8. According to the passage, which of the following statements concerning the dictation of punctuation is CORRECT? 8.____
   A

   A. dictator may use incorrect punctuation to create a desired style

B. dictator should indicate all punctuation
C. stenographer should know how to punctuate based on the pauses and tones of the dictator
D. stenographer should not type any punctuation if it has not been dictated to her

9. According to the passage, how should secretaries handle grammatical errors in a dictation?
Secretaries should

   A. *not correct* grammatical errors unless the dictator is aware that this is being done
   B. *correct* grammatical errors by having the dictator repeat the line with proper pauses
   C. *correct* grammatical errors if they have checked the correctness in a grammar book
   D. *correct* grammatical errors based on their own good sense

10. If a stenographer is confused about the method of spacing and indenting of a report which has just been dictated to her, she GENERALLY should

    A. do the best she can
    B. ask the dictator to explain what she should do
    C. try to improve her ability to understand dictated material
    D. accept the fact that her stenographic ability is not adequate

11. In the last line of the first paragraph, the word *mediocre* means MOST NEARLY

    A. superior   B. disregarded
    C. respected   D. second-rate

12. Assume that is is your responsibility to schedule meetings for your supervisor, who believes in starting these meetings strictly on time. He has told you to schedule separate meetings with Mr. Smith and Ms. Jones, which will last approximately 20 minutes each. You have told Mr. Smith to arrive at 10:00 A.M. and Ms. Jones at 10:30 A.M. Your supervisor will have an hour of free time at 11:00 A.M. At 10:25 A.M., Mr. Smith arrives and states that there was a train delay, and he is sorry that he is late. Ms. Jones has not yet arrived. You do not know who Mr. Smith and Ms. Jones are or what the meetings will be about.
Of the following, the BEST course of action for you to take is to

    A. send Mr. Smith in to see your supervisor; and when Ms. Jones arrives, tell her that your supervisor's first meeting will take more time than he expected
    B. tell Mr. Smith that your supervisor has a meeting at 10:30 A.M. and that you will have to reschedule his meeting for another day
    C. check with your supervisor to find out if he would prefer to see Mr. Smith immediately or at 11:00 A.M.
    D. encourage your supervisor to meet with Mr. Smith immediately because Mr. Smith's late arrival was not intentional

13. Assume that you have been told by your boss not to let anyone disturb him for the rest of the afternoon unless absolutely necessary since he has to complete some urgent work. His supervisor, who is the bureau chief, telephones and asks to speak to him.
The BEST course of action for you to take is to

A. ask the bureau chief if he can leave a message
B. ask your boss if he can take the call
C. tell the bureau chief that your boss is out
D. tell your boss that his instructions will get you into trouble

14. Which one of the following is the MOST advisable procedure for a stenographer to follow when a dictator asks her to make extra copies of dictated material?

    A. Note the number of copies required at the beginning of the notes.
    B. Note the number of copies required at the end of the notes.
    C. Make a mental note of the number of copies required to be made.
    D. Make a checkmark beside the notes to serve as a reminder that extra copies are required.

15. Suppose that, as you are taking shorthand notes, the dictator tells you that the sentence he has just dictated is to be deleted.
    Of the following, the BEST thing for you to do is to

    A. place the correction in the left-hand margin next to the deleted sentence
    B. write the word *delete* over the sentence and place the correction on a separate page for corrections
    C. erase the sentence and use that available space for the correction
    D. draw a line through the sentence and begin the correction on the next available line

16. Assume that your supervisor, who normally dictates at a relatively slow rate, begins dictating to you very rapidly. You find it very difficult to keep up at this speed. Which one of the following is the BEST action to take in this situation?

    A. Ask your supervisor to dictate more slowly since you are having difficulty.
    B. Continue to take the dictation at the fast speed and fill in the blanks later.
    C. Interrupt your supervisor with a question about the dictation, hoping that when she begins again it will be slower.
    D. Refuse to take the dictation unless given at the speed indicated in your job description.

17. Assume that you have been asked to put a heading on the second, third, and fourth pages of a four-page letter to make sure they can be identified in case they are separated from the first page.
    Which of the following is it LEAST important to include in such a heading?

    A. Date of the letter
    B. Initials of the typist
    C. Name of the person to whom the letter is addressed
    D. Number of the page

18. Which one of the following is NOT generally accepted when dividing words at the end of a line?
    Dividing

    A. a hyphenated word at the hyphen
    B. a word immediately after the prefix
    C. a word immediately before the suffix
    D. proper names between syllables

19. In the preparation of a business letter which has two enclosures, the MOST generally accepted of the following procedures to follow is to type 19.____

    A. *See Attached Items* one line below the last line of the body of the letter
    B. *See Attached Enclosures* to the left of the signature
    C. *Enclosures 2* at the left margin below the signature line
    D. nothing on the letter to indicate enclosures since it will be obvious to the reader that there are enclosures in the envelope

20. Standard rules for typing spacing have developed through usage. According to these rules, one space is left AFTER 20.____

    A. a comma
    B. every sentence
    C. a colon
    D. an opening parenthesis

KEY (CORRECT ANSWERS)

1.	C	11.	D
2.	D	12.	C
3.	B	13.	B
4.	A	14.	A
5.	C	15.	D
6.	A	16.	A
7.	B	17.	B
8.	C	18.	D
9.	A	19.	C
10.	B	20.	A

EXAMINATION SECTION
TEST 1

ABBREVIATIONS

DIRECTIONS: Write the meaning of each of the following abbreviations.

1. NOMA
2. w.f.
3. W/B
4. c.i.f.
5. q.v.
6. e.g.
7. op. cit.
8. R/D
9. c.l.
10. ibid.
11. B/S
12. Cr.
13. B/L
14. avoir.
15. assn.

1.____
2.____
3.____
4.____
5.____
6.____
7.____
8.____
9.____
10.____
11.____
12.____
13.____
14.____
15.____

KEY (CORRECT ANSWERS)

1. National Office Management Association
2. wrong font
3. Way Bill
4. cost, insurance, freight
5. which see
6. for example
7. in the work cited
8. Rural Delivery
9. carload
10. in the same place
11. bill of sale
12. credit
13. bill of lading
14. avoirdupois
15. association

TEST 2

PRONUNCIATION

DIRECTIONS: Select the letter of the correct pronunciation. *PRINT THE LETTER OF THE CORRECT ANSWER IN THE SPACE AT THE RIGHT.*

1. NOXIOUS   1.____

    A. nŏk′ shus   B. nō′ shus   C. nŏks′ ē us

2. GENERALLY   2.____

    A. jĕn′ er al i   B. jĕn′ er li   C. jĕn′ ra li

3. HESITATE   3.____

    A. hėz′ i tāt   B. hĕz′ tāt   C. hĕs′ i tāt

4. THEATER   4.____

    A. thē ā′ ter   B. thē′ ȧ ter   C. thē ăt′ er

5. DEFINITELY   5.____

    A. dĕf′ nĭt li   B. dĕf ĭ nĭt′ li   C. dĕf′ ĭ nĭt li

6. ROOSEVELT   6.____

    A. Rō′ zĕ velt   B. Rōz velt′   C. Roōs′ velt

7. LIBRARY   7.____

    A. lī′ bĕr i   B. lī brăr′ i   C. lī′ brĕr i

8. PATHOS   8.____

    A. pāth′ ōs   B. pā′ thōs   C. pȧ thōs′

9. IRREVOCABLE   9.____

    A. i′ rĕv o ka b'l   B. i rĕv′ o ka b'l   C. ir rē vōk′ a b'l

10. ZOOLOGY   10.____

    A. zo ŏl′ o gy   B. zoo ŏl′ o gy   C. zoo ŏl′ gy

45

KEY (CORRECT ANSWERS)

1. A
2. A
3. A
4. B
5. C

6. A
7. C
8. B
9. B
10. A

———

TEST 3

SPELLING

DIRECTIONS: One word in each lettered group is misspelled. Indicate the letter of the misspelled word in the space at the right.

1. A. questionnaire B. gondoleer 1._____
   C. chandelier D. acquiescence

2. A. surveillence B. surfeit 2._____
   C. vaccinate D. belligerent

3. A. occassionally B. recurrence 3._____
   C. silhouette D. incessant

4. A. transferral B. beneficial 4._____
   C. descendent D. dependent

5. A. separately B. flourescence 5._____
   C. deterrent D. parallel

6. A. acquittal B. enforceable 6._____
   C. counterfeit D. indispensible

7. A. susceptible B. accelarate 7._____
   C. exhilarate D. accommodation

8. A. impedimenta B. collateral 8._____
   C. liason D. epistolary

9. A. inveigle B. panegyric 9._____
   C. reservoir D. manuver

10. A. synopsis B. parephernalia 10._____
    C. affidavit D. subpoena

11. A. grosgrain B. vermilion 11._____
    C. abbatoir D. connoiseur

12. A. gabardine B. camoflage 12._____
    C. hemorrhage D. contraband

13. A. opprobrious B. defalcate 13._____
    C. fiduciery D. recommendations

14. A. nebulous B. necessitate 14._____
    C. impricate D. discrepancy

15. A. discrete B. condesension 15._____
    C. condign D. condiment

16. A. cavalier B. effigy 16._____
    C. legitimatly D. misalliance

17. A. rheumatism B. vaporous 17._____
    C. cannister D. hallucinations

47

18. A. paleonthology   B. octogenarian   18._____
    C. gradient   D. impingement

19. A. fusilade   B. fusilage   19._____
    C. ensilage   D. desiccate

20. A. rationale   B. raspberry   20._____
    C. reprobate   D. varigated

21. A. repellent   B. secession   21._____
    C. sebaceous   D. saxaphone

22. A. navel   B. counteresolution 22._____
    C. marginalia   D. perceptible

23. A. Hammerskjold   B. Nehru   23._____
    C. U Thamt   D. Khrushchev

24. A. perculate   B. periwinkle   24._____
    C. perigee   D. retrogression

25. A. buccaneer   B. tobacco   25._____
    C. Buffalo   D. oscilate

KEY (CORRECT ANSWERS)

1. B	11. D
2. A	12. B
3. A	13. C
4. B	14. C
5. B	15. B
6. D	16. C
7. B	17. C
8. C	18. A
9. D	19. A
10. B	20. D

21. D
22. B
23. C
24. A
25. D

TEST 4

SYLLABIFICATION

DIRECTIONS: For each word listed below, one CORRECT syllabication is shown. Indicate the CORRECT choice in the space at the right.

1. A. rep er cus sion   B. re per cus sion   1._____
   C. rep er cuss ion   D. re perc us sion

2. A. corr es pon dence   B. cor resp on dence   2._____
   C. cor re spond ence   D. cor res pond ence

3. A. sup er in ten dent   B. su per in ten dent   3._____
   C. su per int end ent   D. su per in tend ent

4. A. ac com mo date   B. acc om mod ate   4._____
   C. acc omm o date   D. ac com mod ate

5. A. ac know ledge   B. ac knowl edge   5._____
   C. ack nowl edge   D. ack now ledge

6. A. aud it or ium   B. au dit or ium   6._____
   C. aud i tor i um   D. au di to ri um

7. A. hosp i tal ize   B. hos pit a lize   7._____
   C. hosp it al ize   D. hos pi tal ize

8. A. du pli ca tion   B. dup lic a tion   8._____
   C. du plic a tion   D. dup li ca tion

9. A. re cap i tu late   B. rec ap it u late   9._____
   C. re ca pi tu late   D. re ca pit u late

10. A. com plim en ta ry   B. com pli men ta ry   10._____
    C. comp lim ent ar y   D. comp li ment a ry

KEY (CORRECT ANSWERS)

1. B   6. D
2. C   7. D
3. D   8. A
4. A   9. A
5. B   10. B

TEST 5

USAGE

DIRECTIONS: In each of the following groups of sentences, there are three sentences which are correct and one which is incorrect because it contains an error in grammar, usage, diction, or punctuation. Indicate the letter of the INCORRECT sentence in the space at the right.

1. A. There was, in the first place, no indication that a crime had been committed. 1.____
   B. She is taller than any other member of the class.
   C. She decided to leave the book lay on the table.
   D. Haven't you any film in stock at this time?

2. A. Why do you still object to him coming with us to the party? 2.____
   B. If I were you, I should wait for them.
   C. If I were ten years older, I should like this kind of job.
   D. I shall go if you desire it.

3. A. Swimming in the pool, the water looked green. 3.____
   B. His speech is so precise as to seem affected.
   C. I would like to go overseas.
   D. We read each other's letters.

4. A. It must be here somewhere. 4.____
   B. The reason is that there is no bread.
   C. Of all other cities, New York is the largest.
   D. The sand was very warm at the beach.

5. A. If he were wealthy, he would build a hospital for the poor. 5.____
   B. I shall insist that he obey you.
   C. They saw that it was him.
   D. What kind of cactus is this one?

6. A. Because they had been trained for emergencies, the assault did not catch them by surprise. 6.____
   B. They divided the loot between the four of them in proportion to their efforts.
   C. The number of strikes is gradually diminishing.
   D. Between acts we went out to the lobby for a brief chat.

7. A. Through a ruse, the prisoners affected their escape from the concentration camp. 7.____
   B. Constant exposure to danger has affected his mind.
   C. Her affected airs served to alienate her from her friends.
   D. Her vivacity was an affectation.

8. A. It is difficult to recollect that life was like before the war. 8.____
   B. Will each of the pupils please hand their home work in?
   C. There are fewer serious mistakes in this pamphlet than I had thought.
   D. LEAVE HER TO HEAVEN is the title of a novel by Ben Ames Williams.

9. A. I was too greatly relieved to be able to say anything.
    B. These insignia date back to ancient Roman times.
    C. We observed a strange phenomenon; the house seemed to sway in the wind and to tremble like a leaf.
    D. It would be much more preferable if you were no longer seen in his company.

10. A. At this point we were faced with only three alternatives: to push on, to remain where we were, or to return to the village.
    B. We had no choice but to forgive so venial a sin.
    C. In their new picture, the Warners are flouting tradition.
    D. Photographs taken revealed that 2.5 square miles had been burned.

11. A. Please send me this data at your earliest convenience.
    B. The loss of their material proved a severe handicap.
    C. My principal objection to this plan is that it is impracticable.
    D. The doll has lain in the rain all evening.

12. A. I had expected to see my brother.
    B. He expected to have seen his brother.
    C. I hoped to see you do better.
    D. It was his duty to assist our friend.

13. A. He asked whether he might write to his friends.
    B. There are many problems which must be solved before we can be assured of world peace.
    C. Each person with whom I talked expressed his opinion freely.
    D. Holding on to my saddle with all my strength the horse galloped down the road at a terrifying pace.

14. A. Which is the youngest of the two sisters?
    B. I am determined to finish the work before Saturday.
    C. It is difficult to see why the problems were not correctly solved.
    D. I have never met a more interesting person.

15. A. Of all my friends he is the one on whom I can most surely depend.
    B. We value the Constitution because of it's guarantee to freedom.
    C. The audience was deeply stirred by the actor's performance.
    D. Give the book to whoever comes into the room first.

16. A. There is no danger of him being elected.
    B. There is no doubt of his election.
    C. John and he are to be the speakers.
    D. John and she are to be the speakers.

17. A. Everything was in order: the paper ruled, the pencils sharpened,
    B. Neither John nor Peter were able to attend the reception.
    C. In April the streets which had been damaged by cold weather were repaired by the workmen.
    D. You may lend my book to the pupil who you think will enjoy it most.

18. A. He fidgeted, like most children do, while the grown-ups were discussing the problem.
     B. I won't go unless you go with me.
     C. Sitting beside the charred ruins of his cabin, the frontiersman told us the story of the attack.
     D. Certainly there can be no objection to the boys' working on a volunteer basis.

19. A. After graduating high school, he obtained a position as a runner in Wall Street.
     B. Last night, in a radio address, the President urged us to subscribe to the Red Cross.
     C. In the evening, light spring rain cooled the streets.
     D. "Un-American" is a word which has been used even by those whose sympathies may well have been pro-Nazi.

20. A. It is hard to conceive of their not doing good work.
     B. Who won - you or I?
     C. He having read the speech caused much comment.
     D. Their finishing the work proves that it can be done.

21. A. The congregation was dismissed.
     B. The congregation were deeply moved by the sermon.
     C. What kind of automobile is that?
     D. His explanation and mine agree.

22. A. Them that honor me I will honor.
     B. They that believe in me shall be rewarded.
     C. Who did you see at the meeting?
     D. Whom are you writing to?

23. A. Our course of study should not be different now than it was five years ago.
     B. I cannot deny myself the pleasure of publicly thanking the mayor for his actions.
     C. The article on "Morale" has appeared in the Times Literary Supplement.
     D. He died of tuberculosis contracted during service with the Allied Forces.

24. A. If it wasn't for a lucky accident, he would still be an office-clerk.
     B. It is evident that teachers need help.
     C. Rolls of postage stamps may be bought at stationery stores.
     D. Addressing machines are used by firms that publish magazines.

25. A. We have many films in stock at the present time.
     B. Which is the youngest of the two sisters?
     C. "I have nothing further to say," he cried.
     D. The children were dismissed.

KEY (CORRECT ANSWERS)

1. C
2. A
3. A
4. C
5. C

6. B
7. A
8. B
9. D
10. B

11. A
12. B
13. D
14. A
15. B

16. A
17. B
18. A
19. A
20. C

21. C
22. C
23. A
24. A
25. B

TEST 6

VOCABULARY

DIRECTIONS: Select the word or phrase NEAREST in meaning or MOST CLEARLY related to the capitalized word. *PRINT THE LETTER OF THE CORRECT ANSWER IN THE SPACE AT THE RIGHT.*

1. ADMONITORY 1.____
    - A. gloomy
    - B. death-dealing
    - C. terrifying
    - D. warning

2. ANENT 2.____
    - A. against
    - B. adjoining
    - C. presently
    - D. in regard to

3. BRUIT 3.____
    - A. to boil
    - B. to spread abroad
    - C. to ponder
    - D. to injure or butcher

4. CATEGORICAL 4.____
    - A. philosphical
    - B. argumentative
    - C. loud
    - D. positive and unequivocal

5. CEREBRATE 5.____
    - A. to enjoy
    - B. to honor
    - C. to tremble
    - D. to think

6. CINCTURE 6.____
    - A. a division or separation
    - B. a job that involves no real work
    - C. a guarantee
    - D. a belt or girdle

7. CLAQUE 7.____
    - A. a castanet
    - B. a clannish set of persons
    - C. a foolish remark
    - D. hired applauders in a theater

8. COGNATE 8.____
    - A. well informed
    - B. inborn or inherent
    - C. secondary or subordinate
    - D. coming from the same source or root

9. CRUX 9.____
    - A. a laboratory report
    - B. cleavage
    - C. a problem
    - D. the pivotal point

10. DECREPITUDE

    A. awkwardness
    B. carelessness
    C. enfeeblement
    D. lowered morals

11. DEMISE

    A. modesty
    B. death
    C. doubt
    D. forgetfulness

12. DOUR

    A. very dark   B. sullen   C. strong   D. enraged

13. DUDGEON

    A. a club-like weapon
    B. a dark prison
    C. sulky displeasure
    D. crudeness

14. ECLECTIC

    A. one-sided
    B. chosen from various sources
    C. indispensable
    D. extremely particular

15. EXTANT

    A. long drawn out
    B. still existing
    C. far-reaching
    D. prominent

16. FALLACIOUS

    A. trivial   B. obscene   C. misleading   D. hopeless

17. FONT

    A. source   B. wisdom   C. folly   D. a pulpit

18. FRONDS

    A. prongs
    B. decorative borders
    C. thick branches
    D. leaves of a palm tree

19. IMPERMEABLE

    A. temporary
    B. set in one's opinions
    C. not permitting passage
    D. dependable

20. INFRACTION

    A. a violation
    B. a small part of anything
    C. unruliness
    D. a loud noise

21. INTERNECINE

    A. involving mutual slaughter
    B. a bodily organ
    C. internal
    D. between relatives

22. LOGISTICS
    A. a branch of mathematics
    B. the science of military supplies
    C. the art of reasoning
    D. a branch of word study

23. MENDACIOUS
    A. enraged   B. revengeful   C. bragging   D. lying

24. METE
    A. to come up to or touch   B. to agree with
    C. to allot   D. to challenge

25. PALPABLE
    A. finely ground   B. easily persuaded
    C. trembling   D. obvious and evident

26. PARLANCE
    A. sophistication   B. calmness
    C. mode of speech   D. talkativeness

27. PLACATORY
    A. stubborn   B. enraging
    C. designed to appease   D. sluggish

28. POLYGLOT
    A. confused
    B. piggish
    C. expressed in many languages
    D. ugly-looking

29. PREFATORY
    A. prepared in advance   B. chosen above other things
    C. preliminary   D. spoken on the side

30. PROBITY
    A. the establishment of a fact
    B. inquisitiveness
    C. tested virtue
    D. good taste

31. REDOUBT
    A. indecision   B. courage
    C. a stronghold   D. an aqueduct

32. REDUNDANT
    A. undulating   B. superfluous
    C. glorious   D. bounding

33. REPREHEND

   A. to reprove sharply
   C. to be disgusted
   B. to grow angry
   D. to remind one of something

34. REPRISALS

   A. surprises
   C. sharp reproofs
   B. rewards
   D. retaliations

35. ROISTER

   A. tease
   C. make a list of names
   B. revel boisterously
   D. boast

36. SCINTILLA

   A. tinsel
   C. a speck
   B. wit
   D. a brilliant surface

37. SENESCENT

   A. nascent
   C. aging
   B. befitting
   D. bursting

38. SEQUENTIAL

   A. servile
   C. following in order
   B. important
   D. trivial

39. SHARDS

   A. shavings
   C. broken remains
   B. huge slabs of stone
   D. vegetables

40. STEPPE

   A. a platform
   C. woodland
   B. a treeless plain
   D. mountainous country

41. SUPINE

   A. limber
   C. bent over
   B. lying on the back
   D. doubtful

42. TEMERARIOUS

   A. rashly venturous
   C. wicked
   B. delaying
   D. cowardly

43. TERRAIN

   A. a soup bowl
   C. an area of ground
   B. fear
   D. glazed pottery

44. TITILLATE

   A. be frightened
   C. excite agreeably
   B. dress in party clothes
   D. flatter

45. TUTELARY   45.____
    A. pertaining to a guardian   B. pertaining to criticism
    C. extremely strict   D. pertaining to teaching

46. VERNAL   46.____
    A. long drawn out   B. aged
    C. of the spring   D. truthful

47. VORACIOUS   47.____
    A. noisily enthusiastic   B. savage
    C. truthful   D. greedy

48. IMPERVIOUS   48.____
    A. impenetrable   B. impetuous
    C. easily harmed   D. soaking wet

49. ADMONITION   49.____
    A. adjustment   B. adjournment   C. warning   D. monitor

50. ARDENT   50.____
    A. fervid   B. gay   C. savage   D. untamed

KEY (CORRECT ANSWERS)

1. D	11. B	21. A	31. C	41. B
2. D	12. B	22. A	32. B	42. A
3. B	13. C	23. D	33. A	43. C
4. D	14. B	24. C	34. D	44. C
5. D	15. B	25. D	35. B	45. A
6. D	16. C	26. C	36. C	46. C
7. D	17. A	27. C	37. C	47. D
8. D	18. D	28. C	38. C	48. A
9. C	19. C	29. C	39. C	49. C
10. C	20. A	30. C	40. B	50. A

SPELLING
EXAMINATION SECTION
TEST 1

DIRECTIONS: Each question or incomplete statement is followed by several suggested answers or completions. Select the one that BEST answers the question or completes the statement. *PRINT THE LETTER OF THE CORRECT ANSWER IN THE SPACE AT THE RIGHT.*

Questions 1-5.

DIRECTIONS: Questions 1 through 5 consist of four words. Indicate the letter of the word that is CORRECTLY spelled.

1. A. harassment B. harrasment
   C. harasment D. harrassment 1.____

2. A. maintainance B. maintenence
   C. maintainence D. maintenance 2.____

3. A. comparable B. comprable
   C. comparible D. commparable 3.____

4. A. suficient B. sufficiant
   C. sufficient D. suficiant 4.____

5. A. fairly B. fairley C. farely D. fairlie 5.____

Questions 6-10.

DIRECTIONS: Questions 6 through 10 consist of four words. Indicate the letter of the word that is INCORRECTLY spelled.

6. A. pallor B. ballid C. ballet D. pallid 6.____

7. A. urbane B. surburbane
   C. interurban D. urban 7.____

8. A. facial B. physical C. fiscle D. muscle 8.____

9. A. interceed B. benefited
   C. analogous D. altogether 9.____

10. A. seizure B. irrelevant
    C. inordinate D. dissapproved 10.____

KEY (CORRECT ANSWERS)

1. A
2. D
3. A
4. C
5. A
6. B
7. B
8. C
9. A
10. D

TEST 2

DIRECTIONS: Each of Questions 1 through 15 consists of two words preceded by the letters A and B. In each question, one of the words may be spelled INCORRECTLY or both words may be spelled CORRECTLY. If one of the words in a question is spelled INCORRECTLY, print in the space at the right the capital letter preceding the INCORRECTLY spelled word. If both words are spelled CORRECTLY, print the letter C.

1. A. easely   B. readily   1.____
2. A. pursue   B. decend   2.____
3. A. measure   B. laboratory   3.____
4. A. exausted   B. traffic   4.____
5. A. discussion   B. unpleasant   5.____
6. A. campaign   B. murmer   6.____
7. A. guarantee   B. sanatary   7.____
8. A. communication   B. safty   8.____
9. A. numerus   B. celebration   9.____
10. A. nourish   B. begining   10.____
11. A. courious   B. witness   11.____
12. A. undoubtedly   B. thoroughly   12.____
13. A. accessible   B. artifical   13.____
14. A. feild   B. arranged   14.____
15. A. admittence   B. hastily   15.____

KEY (CORRECT ANSWERS)

1.	A	6.	B	11.	A
2.	B	7.	B	12.	C
3.	C	8.	B	13.	B
4.	A	9.	A	14.	A
5.	C	10.	B	15.	A

TEST 3

DIRECTIONS: In each of the following sentences, one word is misspelled. Following each sentence is a list of four words taken from the sentence. Indicate the letter of the word which is MISSPELLED in the sentence. *PRINT THE LETTER OF THE CORRECT ANSWER IN THE SPACE AT THE RIGHT.*

1. The placing of any inflammable substance in any building, or the placing of any device or contrivance capable of producing fire, for the purpose of causing a fire is an attempt to burn.
    A. inflammable
    B. substance
    C. device
    D. contrivence

    1._____

2. The word *break* also means obtaining an entrance into a building by any artifice used for that purpose, or by collussion with any person therein.
    A. obtaining
    B. entrance
    C. artifice
    D. colussion

    2._____

3. Any person who with intent to provoke a breech of the peace causes a disturbance or is offensive to others may be deemed to have committed disorderly conduct.
    A. breech
    B. disturbance
    C. offensive
    D. committed

    3._____

4. When the offender inflicts a grevious harm upon the person from whose possession, or in whose presence, property is taken, he is guilty of robbery.
    A. offender
    B. grevious
    C. possession
    D. presence

    4._____

5. A person who wilfuly encourages or advises another person in attempting to take the latter's life is guilty of a felony.
    A. wilfuly
    B. encourages
    C. advises
    D. attempting

    5._____

6. He maliciously demurred to an ajournment of the proceedings.
    A. maliciously
    B. demurred
    C. ajournment
    D. proceedings

    6._____

7. His innocence at that time is irrelevant in view of his more recent villianous demeanor.
    A. innocence
    B. irrelevant
    C. villianous
    D. demeanor

    7._____

8. The mischievous boys aggrevated the annoyance of their neighbor.
    A. mischievous
    B. aggrevated
    C. annoyance
    D. neighbor

    8._____

2 (#3)

9. While his perseverence was commendable, his judgment was debatable. 9.____
   A. perseverence B. commendable
   C. judgment D. debatable

10. He was hoping the appeal would facilitate his aquittal. 10.____
    A. hoping B. appeal
    C. facilitate D. aquittal

11. It would be preferable for them to persue separate courses. 11.____
    A. preferable B. persue
    C. separate D. courses

12. The litigant was complimented on his persistance and achievement. 12.____
    A. litigant B. complimented
    C. persistance D. achievement

13. Ocassionally there are discrepancies in the descriptions of miscellaneous items. 13.____
    A. ocassionally B. discrepancies
    C. descriptions D. miscellaneous

14. The councilmanic seargent-at-arms enforced the prohibition. 14.____
    A. councilmanic B. seargeant-at-arms
    C. enforced D. prohibition

15. The teacher had an ingenious device for maintaining attendance. 15.____
    A. ingenious B. device
    C. maintaning D. attendance

16. A worrysome situation has developed as a result of the assessment that absenteeism is increasing despite our conscientious efforts. 16.____
    A. worrysome B. assessment
    C. absenteeism D. conscientious

17. I concurred with the credit manager that it was practicable to charge purchases on a biennial basis, and the company agreed to adhear to this policy. 17.____
    A. concurred B. practicable
    C. biennial D. adhear

18. The pastor was chagrined and embarassed by the irreverent conduct of one of his parishioners. 18.____
    A. chagrined B. embarassed
    C. irreverent D. parishioners

19. His inate seriousness was belied by his flippant demeanor. 19.____
    A. inate B. belied
    C. flippant D. demeanor

20. It was exceedingly regrettable that the excessive number of challenges in the court delayed the start of the trial.
    A. exceedingly
    B. regrettable
    C. excessive
    D. challanges

KEY (CORRECT ANSWERS)

1. D   11. B
2. D   12. C
3. A   13. A
4. B   14. B
5. A   15. C

6. C   16. A
7. C   17. D
8. B   18. B
9. A   19. A
10. D   20. D

TEST 4

Questions 1-11.

DIRECTIONS: Each question consists of three words in each question, one of the words may be spelled incorrectly or all three may be spelled correctly. For each question if one of the words is spelled INCORRECTLY, write the letter of the incorrect word in the space at the right. If all three words are spelled CORRECTLY, write the letter D in the space at the right.

SAMPLE I: (A) guide   (B) departmint   (C) stranger
SAMPLE II: (A) comply   (B) valuable   (C) window
In Sample I, departmint is incorrect. It should be spelled department. Therefore, B is the answer.
In Sample II, all three words are spelled correctly. Therefore, D is the answer.

1.	A. argument	B. reciept	C. complain			1.____
2.	A. sufficient	B. postpone	C. visible			2.____
3.	A. expirience	B. dissatisly	C. alternate			3.____
4.	A. occurred	B. noticable	C. appendix			4.____
5.	A. anxious	B. guarantee	C. calendar			5.____
6.	A. sincerely	B. affectionately	C. truly			6.____
7.	A. excellant	B. verify	C. important			7.____
8.	A. error	B. quality	C. enviroment			8.____
9.	A. exercise	B. advance	C. pressure			9.____
10.	A. citizen	B. expence	C. memory			10.____
11.	A. flexable	B. focus	C. forward			11.____

Questions 12-15.

DIRECTIONS: Each of Questions 12 through 15 consists of a group of four words. Examine each group carefully; then in the space at the right, indicate
A. if only one word in the group is spelled correctly
B. if two words in the group are spelled correctly
C. if three words in the group are spelled correctly
D. if all four words in the group are spelled correctly

12. Wendsday, particular, similar, hunderd   12.____

65

13. realize, judgment, opportunities, consistent   13._____

14. equel, principle, assistense, committee   14._____

15. simultaneous, privilege, advise, ocassionaly   15._____

KEY (CORRECT ANSWERS)

1.	B	6.	D	11.	A
2.	D	7.	A	12.	B
3.	A	8.	C	13.	D
4.	B	9.	D	14.	A
5.	C	10.	B	15.	C

TEST 5

DIRECTIONS: Each of Questions 1 through 15 consists of two words preceded by the letters A and B. In each item, one of the words may be spelled INCORRECTLY or both words may be spelled CORRECTLY. If one of the words in a question is spelled INCORRECTLY, print in the space at the right the letter preceding the INCORRECTLY spelled word. If bot words are spelled CORRECTLY, print the letter C.

1.	A. justified	B. offering	1.____
2.	A. predjudice	B. license	2.____
3.	A. label	B. pamphlet	3.____
4.	A. bulletin	B. physical	4.____
5.	A. assure	B. exceed	5.____
6.	A. advantagous	B. evident	6.____
7.	A. benefit	B. occured	7.____
8.	A. acquire	B. graditude	8.____
9.	A. amenable	B. boundry	9.____
10.	A. deceive	B. voluntary	10.____
11.	A. imunity	B. conciliate	11.____
12.	A. acknoledge	B. presume	12.____
13.	A. substitute	B. prespiration	13.____
14.	A. reputable	B. announce	14.____
15.	A. luncheon	B. wretched	15.____

KEY (CORRECT ANSWERS)

1.	C	6.	A	11.	A
2.	A	7.	B	12.	A
3.	C	8.	B	13.	B
4.	C	9.	B	14.	A
5.	C	10.	C	15.	C

TEST 6

DIRECTIONS: Questions 1 through 15 contain lists of words, one of which is misspelled. Indicate the MISSPELLED word in each group. *PRINT THE LETTER OF THE CORRECT ANSWER IN THE SPACE AT THE RIGHT.*

1. A. felony B. lacerate 1.____
   C. cancellation D. seperate

2. A. batallion B. beneficial 2.____
   C. miscellaneous D. secretary

3. A. camouflage B. changeable 3.____
   C. embarrass D. inoculate

4. A. beneficial B. disasterous 4.____
   C. incredible D. miniature

5. A. auxilliary B. hypocrisy 5.____
   C. phlegm D. vengeance

6. A. aisle B. cemetary 6.____
   C. courtesy D. extraordinary

7. A. crystallize B. innoculate 7.____
   C. eminent D. symmetrical

8. A. judgment B. maintainance 8.____
   C. bouillon D. eery

9. A. isosceles B. ukulele 9.____
   C. mayonaise D. iridescent

10. A. remembrance B. occurence 10.____
    C. correspondence D. countenance

11. A. corpuscles B. mischievous 11.____
    C. batchelor D. bulletin

12. A. terrace B. banister 12.____
    C. concrete D. masonery

13. A. balluster B. gutter 13.____
    C. latch D. bridging

14. A. personnell B. navel 14.____
    C. therefor D. emigrant

15. A. committee B. submiting 15.____
    C. amendment D. electorate

KEY (CORRECT ANSWERS)

1.	D	6.	B	11.	C
2.	A	7.	B	12.	D
3.	C	8.	B	13.	A
4.	B	9.	C	14.	A
5.	A	10.	B	15.	B

TEST 7

Questions 1-5.

DIRECTIONS: Questions 1 through 5 consist of groups of four words. Select answer
A if only one word is spelled correctly in a group
B if TWO words are spelled correctly in a group
C if THREE words are spelled correctly in a group
D if all FOUR words are spelled correctly in a group.

1. counterfeit, embarass, panicky, supercede   1._____
2. benefited, personnel, questionnaire, unparalelled   2._____
3. bankruptcy, describable, proceed, vacuum   3._____
4. handicapped, mispell, offerred, pilgrimmage   4._____
5. corduroy, interfere, privilege, separator   5._____

Questions 6-10.

DIRECTIONS: Questions 6 through 10 consist of four pairs of words each. Some of the words are spelled correctly; others are spelled incorrectly. For each question, indicate in the space at the right the letter preceding that pair of words in which BOTH words are spelled CORRECTLY.

6. A. hygienic, inviegle   B. omniscience, pittance   6._____
   C. plagarize, nullify   D. seargent, perilous

7. A. auxilary, existence   B. pronounciation, accordance   7._____
   C. ignominy, indegence   D. suable, baccalaureate

8. A. discreet, inaudible   B. hypocrisy, currupt   8._____
   C. liquidate, maintainance   D. transparancy, onerous

9. A. facility; stimulent   B. frugel, sanitary   9._____
   C. monetary, prefatory   D. punctileous, credentials

10. A. bankruptsy, perceptible B. disuade, resilient   10._____
    C. exhilerate, expectancy   D. panegyric, disparate

Questions 11-15.

DIRECTIONS: Each question or incomplete statement is followed by several suggested answers or completions. Select the one that BEST answers the question or completes the statement. PRINT THE LETTER OF THE CORRECT ANSWER IN THE SPACE AT THE RIGHT.

11. The silent *e* must be retained when the suffix *–able* is added to the word 11.____
    A. argue   B. love   C. move   D. notice

12. The CORRECTLY spelled word in the choices below is 12.____
    A. kindergarden   B. zylophone
    C. hemorrhage   D. mayonaise

13. Of the following words, the one spelled CORRECTLY is 13.____
    A. begger   B. cemetary
    C. embarassed   D. coyote

14.
    A. dandilion   B. wiry   C. sieze   D. rythmic   14.____

15. A. beligerent   B. anihilation
    C. facetious   D. adversery

KEY (CORRECT ANSWERS)

1.	B	6.	B	11.	D
2.	C	7.	D	12.	C
3.	D	8.	A	13.	D
4.	A	9.	C	14.	B
5.	D	10.	D	15.	C

TEST 8

DIRECTIONS: In each of the following sentences, one word is misspelled. Following each sentence is a list of four words taken from the sentence. Indicate the letter of the word which is MISSPELLED. *PRINT THE LETTER OF THE CORRECT ANSWER IN THE SPACE AT THE RIGHT.*

1. If the administrator attempts to withold information, there is a good likelihood that there will be serious repercussions.
   A. administrator
   B. withold
   C. likelihood
   D. repercussions

   1.____

2. He condescended to apologize, but we felt that a beligerent person should not occupy an influential position.
   A. condescended
   B. apologize
   C. beligerent
   D. influential

   2.____

3. Despite the sporadic delinquent payments of his indebtedness, Mr. Johnson has been an exemplery customer.
   A. sporadic
   B. delinquent
   C. indebtedness
   D. exemplery

   3.____

4. He was appreciative of the support he consistantly acquired, but he felt that he had waited an inordinate length of time for it.
   A. appreciative
   B. consistantly
   C. acquired
   D. inordinate

   4.____

5. Undeniably they benefited from the establishment of a receivership, but the question of statutary limitations remained unresolved.
   A. undeniably
   B. benefited
   C. receivership
   D. statutary

   5.____

6. Mr. Smith profered his hand as an indication that he considered it a viable contract, but Mr. Nelson alluded to the fact that his colleagues had not been consulted.
   A. profered
   B. viable
   C. alluded
   D. colleagues

   6.____

7. The treatments were beneficial according to the optomotrists, and the consensus was that minimal improvement could be expected.
   A. beneficial
   B. optomotrists
   C. consensus
   D. minimal

   7.____

8. Her frivolous manner was unbecoming because the air of solemnity at the cemetery was pervasive.
   A. frivalous
   B. solemnity
   C. cemetery
   D. pervasive

   8.____

9. The clandestine meetings were designed to make the two adversaries more amicable, but they served only to intensify their emnity.
   A. clandestine
   B. adversaries
   C. amicable
   D. emnity

10. Do you think that his innovative ideas and financial acumen will help stabalize the fluctuations of the stock market?
    A. innovative
    B. acumen
    C. stabalize
    D. fluctuations

11. In order to keep a perpetual inventory, you will have to keep an uninterrupted surveillance of all the miscellanious stock.
    A. perpetual
    B. uninterrupted
    C. surveillance
    D. miscellanious

12. She used the art of pursuasion on the children because she found that caustic remarks had no perceptible effect on their behavior.
    A. pursuasion
    B. caustic
    C. perceptible
    D. effect

13. His sacreligious outbursts offended his constituents, and he was summarily removed from office by the City Council.
    A. sacreligious
    B. constituents
    C. summarily
    D. Council

14. They exhorted the contestants to greater efforts, but the exhorbitant costs in terms of energy expended resulted in a feeling of lethargy.
    A. exhorted
    B. contestants
    C. exhorbitant
    D. lethargy

15. Since he was knowledgable about illicit drugs, he was served with a subpoena to appear for the prosecution.
    A. knowledgable
    B. illicit
    C. subpoena
    D. prosecution

16. In spite of his lucid statements, they denigrated his report and decided it should be succintly paraphrased.
    A. lucid
    B. denigrated
    C. succintly
    D. paraphrased

17. The discussion was not germane to the contraversy, but the indicted man's insistence on further talk was allowed.
    A. germane
    B. contraversy
    C. indicted
    D. insistence

18. The legislators were enervated by the distances they had traveled during the election year to fullfil their speaking engagements.
    A. legislators
    B. enervated
    C. traveled
    D. fullfil

19. The plaintiffs' attornies charge the defendant in the case with felonious assault. 19.____
    A. plaintiffs'
    B. attornies
    C. defendant
    D. felonious

20. It is symptomatic of the times that we try to placate all, but a proposal for new forms of disciplinery action was promulgated by the staff. 20.____
    A. symptomatic
    B. placate
    C. disciplinery
    D. promulgated

KEY (CORRECT ANSWERS)

1.	B	11.	D
2.	C	12.	A
3.	D	13.	A
4.	B	14.	C
5.	D	15.	A
6.	A	16.	C
7.	B	17.	B
8.	A	18.	D
9.	D	19.	B
10.	C	20.	C

TEST 9

DIRECTIONS: Each of Questions 1 through 15 consists of a single word which is spelled either correctly or incorrectly. If the word is spelled CORRECTLY, you are to print the letter C (Correct) in the space at the right. If the word is spelled INCORRECTL, you are to print the letter W (Wrong).

1. pospone　　　　　　　　　　　　　　　　　　　　　　　　　　　　　　　　　1.____
2. diffrent　　　　　　　　　　　　　　　　　　　　　　　　　　　　　　　　　2.____
3. height　　　　　　　　　　　　　　　　　　　　　　　　　　　　　　　　　3.____
4. carefully　　　　　　　　　　　　　　　　　　　　　　　　　　　　　　　　4.____
5. ability　　　　　　　　　　　　　　　　　　　　　　　　　　　　　　　　　5.____
6. temper　　　　　　　　　　　　　　　　　　　　　　　　　　　　　　　　　6.____
7. deslike　　　　　　　　　　　　　　　　　　　　　　　　　　　　　　　　　7.____
8. seldem　　　　　　　　　　　　　　　　　　　　　　　　　　　　　　　　　8.____
9. alcohol　　　　　　　　　　　　　　　　　　　　　　　　　　　　　　　　　9.____
10. expense　　　　　　　　　　　　　　　　　　　　　　　　　　　　　　　　10.____
11. vegatable　　　　　　　　　　　　　　　　　　　　　　　　　　　　　　　11.____
12. dispensary　　　　　　　　　　　　　　　　　　　　　　　　　　　　　　12.____
13. specemin　　　　　　　　　　　　　　　　　　　　　　　　　　　　　　　13.____
14. allowance　　　　　　　　　　　　　　　　　　　　　　　　　　　　　　14.____
15. exersise　　　　　　　　　　　　　　　　　　　　　　　　　　　　　　　15.____

KEY (CORRECT ANSWERS)

1.	W	6.	C	11.	W
2.	W	7.	W	12.	C
3.	C	8.	W	13.	W
4.	C	9.	C	14.	C
5.	C	10.	C	15.	W

TEST 10

DIRECTIONS: Each of Questions 1 through 10 consists of four words, one of which may be spelled incorrectly or all four words may be spelled correctly. If one of the words in a question is spelled incorrectly, print in the space at the right the capital letter preceding the word which is spelled INCORRECTLY. If all four words are spelled CORRECTLY, print the letter E.

1. A. dismissal B. collateral 1.____
   C. leisure   D. proffession

2. A. subsidary B. outrageous 2.____
   C. liaison   D. assessed

3. A. already   B. changeable 3.____
   C. mischevous D. cylinder

4. A. supersede B. deceit   4.____
   C. dissension D. imminent

5. A. arguing   B. contagious 5.____
   C. comparitive D. accessible

6. A. indelible B. existance   6.____
   C. presumptuous D. mileage

7. A. extention B. aggregate   7.____
   C. sustenance D. gratuitous

8. A. interrogate B. exaggeration 8.____
   C. vacillate D. moreover

9. A. parallel   B. derogatory 9.____
   C. admissible D. appellate

10. A. safety   B. cumalative 10.____
    C. disappear D. usable

KEY (CORRECT ANSWERS)

1. D   6. B
2. A   7. A
3. C   8. E
4. E   9. C
5. C   10. B

TEST 11

DIRECTIONS: Each of questions 1 through 10 consists of four words, one of which may be spelled incorrectly or all four words may be spelled correctly. If one of the words in a question is spelled INCORRECTLY, print in the space at the right the capital letter preceding the word which is spelled incorrectly. If all four words are spelled CORRECTLY, print the letter E.

1. A. vehicular   B. gesticulate   1._____
   C. manageable   D. fullfil

2. A. inovation   B. onerous   2._____
   C. chastise   D. irresistible

3. A. familiarize   B. dissolution   3._____
   C. oscillate   D. superflous

4. A. census   B. defender   4._____
   C. adherence   D. inconceivable

5. A. voluminous   B. liberalize   5._____
   C. bankrupcy   D. conversion

6. A. justifiable   B. executor   6._____
   C. perpatrate   D. dispelled

7. A. boycott   B. abeyence   7._____
   C. enterprise   D. circular

8. A. spontaineous   B. dubious   8._____
   C. analyze   D. premonition

9. A. intelligible   B. apparently   9._____
   C. genuine   D. crucial

10. A. plentiful   B. ascertain   10._____
    C. carreer   D. preliminary

KEY (CORRECT ANSWERS)

1.	D	6.	C
2.	A	7.	B
3.	D	8.	A
4.	E	9.	E
5.	C	10.	C

TEST 12

DIRECTIONS: Each of questions 1 through 25 consists of four words, one of which may be spelled incorrectly or all four words may be spelled correctly. If one of the words in a question is spelled INCORRECTLY, print in the space at the right the capital letter preceding the word which is spelled incorrectly. If all four words are spelled CORRECTLY, print the letter E.

1. A. temporary B. existance C. complimentary D. altogether 1.____

2. A. privilege B. changeable C. jeopardize D. commitment 2.____

3. A. grievous B. alloted C. outrageous D. mortgage 3.____

4. A. tempermental B. accommodating C. bookkeeping D. panicky 4.____

5. A. auxiliary B. indispensable C. ecstasy D. fiery 5.____

6. A. dissappear B. buoyant C. imminent D. parallel 6.____

7. A. loosly B. medicine C. schedule D. defendant 7.____

8. A. endeavor B. persuade C. retroactive D. desparate 8.____

9. A. usage B. servicable C. disadvantageous D. remittance 9.____

10. A. beneficary B. receipt C. excitable D. implement 10.____

11. A. accompanying B. intangible C. offerred D. movable 11.____

12. A. controlling B. seize C. repetitious D. miscellaneous 12.____

13. A. installation B. accommodation C. consistant D. illuminate 13.____

14. A. incidentaly B. privilege C. apparent D. chargeable 14.____

78

15. A. prevalent   B. serial   15.____
    C. briefly   D. disatisfied

16. A. reciprocal   B. concurrence   16.____
    C. persistence   D. withold

17. A. deferred   B. suing   17.____
    C. fulfilled   D. pursuant

18. A. questionable B. omission   18.____
    C. acknowledgment D. insistent

19. A. guarantee   B. committment   19.____
    C. mitigate   D. publicly

20. A. prerogative   B. apprise   20.____
    C. extrordinary D. continual

21. A. arrogant   B. handicapped   21.____
    C. judicious   D. perennial

22. A. permissable   B. deceive   22.____
    C. innumerable   D. retrieve

23. A. notable   B. allegiance   23.____
    C. reimburse   D. illegal

24. A. wholly   B. disbursement   24.____
    C. hindrance   D. conciliatory

25. A. guidance   B. condemn   25.____
    C. publically   D. coercion

KEY (CORRECT ANSWERS)

1.	B	11.	C
2.	E	12.	E
3.	B	13.	C
4.	A	14.	A
5.	E	15.	D
6.	A	16.	D
7.	A	17.	E
8.	D	18.	A
9.	B	19.	B
10.	A	20.	C

21. E
22. A
23. E
24. E
25. C

PREPARING WRITTEN MATERIAL
EXAMINATION SECTION
TEST 1

DIRECTIONS: Each of the sentences in this test may be classified under one of the following four categories:
- A. Faulty because of incorrect grammar or word usage
- B. Faulty because of incorrect punctuation
- C. Faulty because of incorrect capitalization or incorrect spelling
- D. Correct

Examine each sentence carefully to determine under which of the above four options it is best classified. Then, in the space to the right, print the capital letter preceding the option which is the BEST of the four suggested above. (Note that each faulty sentence contains but one type of error. Consider a sentence to be correct if it contains none of the types of errors mentioned, even though there may be other correct ways of expressing the same thought.)

1. He sent the notice to the clerk who you hired yesterday. 1._____

2. It must be admitted, however that you were not informed of this change. 2._____

3. Only the employee who have served in this grade for at least two years are eligible for promotion. 3._____

4. The work was divided equally between she and Mary. 4._____

5. He thought that you were not available at that time. 5._____

6. When the messenger returns; please give him this package. 6._____

7. The new secretary prepared, typed, addressed, and delivered, the notices. 7._____

8. Walking into the room, his desk can be seen at the rear. 8._____

9. Although John has worked here longer than She, he produces a smaller amount of work. 9._____

10. She said she could of typed this report yesterday. 10._____

11. Neither one of these procedures are adequate for the efficient performance of this task. 11._____

12. The typewriter is the tool of the typist; the cash register, the tool of the cashier. 12._____

13. "The assignment must be completed as soon as possible" said the supervisor. 13.____

14. As you know, office handbooks are issued to all new Employees. 14.____

15. Writing a speech is sometimes easier than to deliver it before an audience. 15.____

16. Mr. Brown our accountant, will audit the accounts next week. 16.____

17. Give the assignment to whomever is able to do it most efficiently. 17.____

18. The supervisor expected either your or I to file these reports. 18.____

KEY (CORRECT ANSWERS)

1.	A	11.	A
2.	B	12.	C
3.	D	13.	B
4.	A	14.	C
5.	D	15.	A
6.	B	16.	B
7.	B	17.	A
8.	A	18.	A
9.	C		
10.	A		

TEST 2

DIRECTIONS: Each of the sentences in this test may be classified under one of the following four categories:
- A. Faulty because of incorrect grammar or word usage
- B. Faulty because of incorrect punctuation
- C. Faulty because of incorrect capitalization or incorrect spelling
- D. Correct

Examine each sentence carefully to determine under which of the above four options it is best classified. Then, in the space to the right, print the capital letter preceding the option which is the BEST of the four suggested above. (Note that each faulty sentence contains but one type of error. Consider a sentence to be correct if it contains none of the types of errors mentioned, even though there may be other correct ways of expressing the same thought.)

1. The fire apparently started in the storeroom, which is usually locked.   1.____
2. On approaching the victim, two bruises were noticed by this officer.   2.____
3. The officer, who was there examined the report with great care.   3.____
4. Each employee in the office had a seperate desk.   4.____
5. All employees including members of the clerical staff, were invited to the lecture.   5.____
6. The suggested Procedure is similar to the one now in use.   6.____
7. No one was more pleased with the new procedure than the chauffeur.   7.____
8. He tried to persaude her to change the procedure.   8.____
9. The total of the expenses charged to petty cash were high.   9.____
10. An understanding between him and I was finally reached.   10.____

KEY (CORRECT ANSWERS)

1.	D	6.	C
2.	A	7.	D
3.	B	8.	C
4.	C	9.	A
5.	B	10.	A

TEST 3

DIRECTIONS: Each of the sentences in this test may be classified under one of the following four categories:
   A. Faulty because of incorrect grammar or word usage
   B. Faulty because of incorrect punctuation
   C. Faulty because of incorrect capitalization or incorrect spelling
   D. Correct

Examine each sentence carefully to determine under which of the above four options it is best classified. Then, in the space to the right, print the capital letter preceding the option which is the BEST of the four suggested above. (Note that each faulty sentence contains but one type of error. Consider a sentence to be correct if it contains none of the types of errors mentioned, even though there may be other correct ways of expressing the same thought.)

1. They told both he and I that the prisoner had escaped.   1._____

2. Any superior officer, who, disregards the just complaint of his subordinates, is remiss in the performance of his duty.   2._____

3. Only those members of the national organization who resided in the Middle West attended the conference in Chicago.   3._____

4. We told him to give the national organization assignment to whoever was available.   4._____

5. Please do not disappoint and embarass us by not appearing in court.   5._____

6. Although the office's speech proved to be entertaining, the topic was not relevent to the main theme of the conference.   6._____

7. In February all new officers attended a training course in which they were learned in their principal duties and the fundamental operating procedure of the department.   7._____

8. I personally seen inmate Jones threaten inmates Smith and Green with bodily harm if they refused to participate in the plot.   8._____

9. To the layman, who on a chance visit to the prison observes everything functioning smoothly, the maintenance of prison discipline may seem to be a relatively easily realizable objective.   9._____

10. The prisoners in cell block fourty were forbidden to sit on the cell cots during the recreation hour.   10._____

KEY (CORRECT ANSWERS)

1. A   6. C
2. B   7. A
3. C   8. A
4. D   9. D
5. C   10. C

TEST 4

DIRECTIONS: Each of the sentences in this test may be classified under one of the following four categories:
- A. Faulty because of incorrect grammar or word usage
- B. Faulty because of incorrect punctuation
- C. Faulty because of incorrect capitalization or incorrect spelling
- D. Correct

Examine each sentence carefully to determine under which of the above four options it is best classified. Then, in the space to the right, print the capital letter preceding the option which is the BEST of the four suggested above. (Note that each faulty sentence contains but one type of error. Consider a sentence to be correct if it contains none of the types of errors mentioned, even though there may be other correct ways of expressing the same thought.)

1. I cannot encourage you any.   1.____
2. You always look well in those sort of clothes.   2.____
3. Shall we go to the park?   3.____
4. The man whome he introduced was Mr. Carey.   4.____
5. She saw the letter laying here this morning.   5.____
6. It should rain before the Afternoon is over.   6.____
7. They have already went home.   7.____
8. That Jackson will be elected is evident.   8.____
9. He does not hardly approve of us.   9.____
10. It was he, who won the prize.   10.____

KEY (CORRECT ANSWERS)

1.	A	6.	C
2.	A	7.	A
3.	D	8.	D
4.	C	9.	A
5.	A	10.	B

TEST 5

DIRECTIONS: Each of the sentences in this test may be classified under one of the following four categories:
- A. Faulty because of incorrect grammar or word usage
- B. Faulty because of incorrect punctuation
- C. Faulty because of incorrect capitalization or incorrect spelling
- D. Correct

Examine each sentence carefully to determine under which of the above four options it is best classified. Then, in the space to the right, print the capital letter preceding the option which is the BEST of the four suggested above. (Note that each faulty sentence contains but one type of error. Consider a sentence to be correct if it contains none of the types of errors mentioned, even though there may be other correct ways of expressing the same thought.)

1. Shall we go to the park.   1._____
2. They are, alike, in this particular way.   2._____
3. They gave the poor man sume food when he knocked on the door.   3._____
4. I regret the loss caused by the error.   4._____
5. The students' will have a new teacher.   5._____
6. They sweared to bring out all the facts.   6._____
7. He decided to open a branch store on 33rd street.   7._____
8. His speed is equal and more than that of a racehorse.   8._____
9. He felt very warm on that Summer day.   9._____
10. He was assisted by his friend, who lives in the next house.   10._____

KEY (CORRECT ANSWERS)

1.	B	6.	A
2.	B	7.	C
3.	C	8.	A
4.	D	9.	C
5.	B	10.	D

TEST 6

DIRECTIONS: Each of the sentences in this test may be classified under one of the following four categories:
- A. Faulty because of incorrect grammar or word usage
- B. Faulty because of incorrect punctuation
- C. Faulty because of incorrect capitalization or incorrect spelling
- D. Correct

Examine each sentence carefully to determine under which of the above four options it is best classified. Then, in the space to the right, print the capital letter preceding the option which is the BEST of the four suggested above. (Note that each faulty sentence contains but one type of error. Consider a sentence to be correct if it contains none of the types of errors mentioned, even though there may be other correct ways of expressing the same thought.)

1. The climate of New York is colder than California. 1._____
2. I shall wait for you on the corner. 2._____
3. Did we see the boy who, we think, is the leader. 3._____
4. Being a modest person, John seldom talks about his invention. 4._____
5. The gang is called the smith street bos. 5._____
6. He seen the man break into the store. 6._____
7. We expected to lay still there for quite a while. 7._____
8. He is considered to be the Leader of his organization. 8._____
9. Although I recieved an invitation, I won't go. 9._____
10. The letter must be here some place. 10._____

KEY (CORRECT ANSWERS)

1.	A	6.	A
2.	D	7.	A
3.	B	8.	C
4.	D	9.	C
5.	C	10.	A

TEST 7

DIRECTIONS: Each of the sentences in this test may be classified under one of the following four categories:
- A. Faulty because of incorrect grammar or word usage
- B. Faulty because of incorrect punctuation
- C. Faulty because of incorrect capitalization or incorrect spelling
- D. Correct

Examine each sentence carefully to determine under which of the above four options it is best classified. Then, in the space to the right, print the capital letter preceding the option which is the BEST of the four suggested above. (Note that each faulty sentence contains but one type of error. Consider a sentence to be correct if it contains none of the types of errors mentioned, even though there may be other correct ways of expressing the same thought.)

1. I though it to be he. 1.____
2. We expect to remain here for a long time. 2.____
3. The committee was agreed. 3.____
4. Two-thirds of the building are finished. 4.____
5. The water was froze. 5.____
6. Everyone of the salesmen must supply their own car. 6.____
7. Who is the author of Gone With the Wind? 7.____
8. He marched on and declaring that he would never surrender. 8.____
9. Who shall I say called? 9.____
10. Everyone has left but they. 10.____

KEY (CORRECT ANSWERS)

1. A   6. A
2. D   7. B
3. D   8. A
4. A   9. D
5. A   10. D

TEST 8

DIRECTIONS: Each of the sentences in this test may be classified under one of the following four categories:
- A. Faulty because of incorrect grammar or word usage
- B. Faulty because of incorrect punctuation
- C. Faulty because of incorrect capitalization or incorrect spelling
- D. Correct

Examine each sentence carefully to determine under which of the above four options it is best classified. Then, in the space to the right, print the capital letter preceding the option which is the BEST of the four suggested above. (Note that each faulty sentence contains but one type of error. Consider a sentence to be correct if it contains none of the types of errors mentioned, even though there may be other correct ways of expressing the same thought.)

1. Who did we give the order to?
2. Send your order in immediately.
3. I believe I paid the Bill.
4. I have not met but one person.
5. Why aren't Tom, and Fred, going to the dance?
6. What reason is there for him not going?
7. The seige of Malta was a tremendous event.
8. I was there yesterday I assure you
9. Your ukulele is better than mine.
10. No one was there only Mary.

KEY (CORRECT ANSWERS)

1.	A	6.	A
2.	D	7.	C
3.	C	8.	B
4.	A	9.	C
5.	B	10.	A

TEST 9

DIRECTIONS: In each of the following groups of sentences, one of the four sentences is faulty in grammar, punctuation, or capitalization. Select the INCORRECT sentence in each case.

1. A. If you had stood at home and done your homework, you would not have failed in arithmetic.
   B. Her affected manner annoyed every member of the audience.
   C. How will the new law affect our income taxes?
   D. The plants were not affected by the long, cold winter, but they succumbed to the drought of summer.

   1.____

2. A. He is one of the most able men who have been in the Senate.
   B. It is he who is to blame for the lamentable mistake.
   C. Haven't you a helpful suggestion to make at this time?
   D. The money was robbed from the blind man's cup.

   2.____

3. A. The amount of children in this school is steadily increasing.
   B. After taking an apple from the table, she went out to play.
   C. He borrowed a dollar from me.
   D. I had hoped my brother would arrive before me.

   3.____

4. A. Whom do you think I hear from every week?
   B. Who do you think is the right man for the job?
   C. Who do you think I found in the room?
   D. He is the man whom we considered a good candidate for the presidency.

   4.____

5. A. Quietly the puppy laid down before the fireplace.
   B. You have made your bed; now lie in it.
   C. I was badly sunburned because I had lain too long in the sun.
   D. I laid the doll on the bed and left the room.

   5.____

KEY (CORRECT ANSWERS)

1. A
2. D
3. A
4. C
5. A

EXAMINATION SECTION
TEST 1

OFFICIAL DICTATION

(175 Words per minute for five (5) minutes)

This Court has granted a writ of certiorari to review a final order of the New York Court of Appeals, which affirmed an order of the Appellate Division of the Supreme Court of the State of New York, First Judicial Department. That order disapproved petitioner's claim that certain sales taxes were due and owing to it by the respondent. The sum in dispute is two thousand, nine hundred and eighty-three dollars, with interest, and the period involved covers the years nineteen seventy-one and nineteen seventy-two.

The sole ground for the rejection of the petitioner's claim by the order under review was that the sales tax law as here applied violated the commerce clause of the federal constitution. The respondent in this proceeding is the Smith Office Machine Company, an Illinois firm engaged in the manufacture and sale of office machines to buyers in all parts of the country. With the Green Adding Machine Company, its wholly owned subsidiary and agent, it maintains offices, workrooms and a stockroom in New York City. There it sells, rents, repairs and services office machines and parts of office machines. Its New York City staff consists of a sales manager and several sales representatives. Only those New York City sales which are filled for the New York Office by shipment from the Illinois factory are the subject of this suit.

The respondent's products are office machines in standard sizes and models, not designed or altered to fill any special orders. The company does not accept any special orders for office machines. A large supply of office machines, with a market value of at least eighty-five thousand dollars, is always kept on hand in its New York City stockrooms. However, the company does not fill its local orders from local stock, but employs an interstate procedure. Orders are taken by the company's New York office and forwarded to the Chicago office. Every order states the model number, style, size and price of each machine sold. The order does not name the place of shipment of the machines, nor is there any evidence that the purchaser knows the place from which the machines are to be shipped to his office. Since the respondent bears the shipping costs and risk of loss, the customer actually purchases the machines in delivered condition.

All orders taken are subject to confirmation by the Chicago office. However, the procedure as to confirmation appears to be largely routine. Prices are fixed by the sales office in New York City on the basis of a standard price list. The trade-in value of old machines is fixed by the sales manager in New York City. There is no evidence that the Chicago office ever fails to confirm, nor is there any evidence that the customer is ever notified of confirmation. As a matter of fact, the order form contains no space for confirmation. The requirement of Chicago confirmation appears to serve no purpose other than to ascertain errors in price quoting and to allow for credit checking.

The respondent packs the machine in a carton and ships it, not to the customer, but to its New York City office. The customer is not concerned at all with this shipment, is not the consignee, is not protected by the insurance, and, consequently, does not pay the freight charges. The respondent must ship the office machine to its New York workroom because the machine on its arrival there is frequently not in a deliverable condition. There is a great deal of breakage in transit which must be repaired in the New York workroom. Even where there has been no breakage, testing and adjusting must be done there. These tasks of testing and adjusting often take three or four days, and it is not until they are finished that the local office can make delivery to the customer.

The contractual obligations of the respondent do not cease with delivery. Each contract of sale requires the company to keep the office machine in good repair for one year from the date of delivery, without charge to the customer. To fulfill this obligation, the respondent renders a free monthly maintenance service of inspection, oiling, and cleaning. When repairs of a substantial nature are needed, the work is done in New York City. While the machine is at the workroom for repair, a loan is made of another machine from the company's stock.

The recital of all these facts serves to show clearly that the tax in question does not interfere with the power reserved to the federal government to regulate interstate commerce. This court has never invalidated a state statute unless it has found that the statute, as a matter of fact, subjected interstate commerce to a greater burden, or to the danger of a greater burden, than would arise if the commerce were not being done. This court has very recently sustained a tax identical with the tax in question in every factual respect in a case involving the same petititioner and this same method of selling and shipping goods across state lines. Therefore, we believe that factual analysis reveals that this tax does not impose a burden upon interstate commerce. The final order and judgment should be reversed.

TEST 2

OFFICIAL DICTATION

(175 Words per minute for five(5) minutes)

The Supreme Court granted the motions made by the plaintiff, George Jones, to strike out the answer, to dismiss the counterclaim and to grant summary judgment. The court then appointed a referee to compute the amount due and owing to the plaintiff. The referee received and considered all the pleadings, including the answer and the bill of particulars submitted by the defendant, Albert Smith, as well as certain receipts. These receipts showed that the defendant had paid a total of ten thousand, nine hundred and eight dollars and forty-nine cents for interest and for amortization of the principal amount of the mortgages as well as for taxes and for the cost of defending an earlier action to foreclose the first mortgage on the property. The referee reported that the total balance due to the plaintiff was eighteen thousand, four hundred and twenty-seven dollars and eighty-five cents. The court granted a judgment for that amount, together with costs and other allowances, and ordered foreclosure and sale of property.

After this judgment had $\underset{X}{\overset{1}{}}$ been granted, the defendant moved for an order to direct a rehearing of his motion to dismiss the complaint and for leave to submit an amended answer. The proposed amended answer, as attached to the moving papers, contained defenses similar to those interposed in the original answer. One new defense, alleging forgiveness by the plaintiff of part of the principal sum due, was offered but rejected by the court because of lack of evidence. In this defense, the defendant, Albert Smith, claimed that a total of three thousand, two hundred and twenty-six dollars had been forgiven by the plaintiff during the period from August, nineteen sixty-six until March, nineteen sixty-eight.

From these orders and the final judgment, the defendant has appealed to this court. During pendency of this appeal, the defendant assigned his entire interest in the property to the White Star Corporation. The date of this assignment was March twelfth, nineteen sixty-nine. Shortly thereafter, Smith attempted to withdraw his answer in the foreclosure action. He also agreed to the entry $\underset{X}{\overset{2}{}}$ of a final judgment and, at the same time, stipulated that he would withdraw his appeal to this court. The motives prompting Albert Smith to this unusual course of conduct are not as yet apparent. The White Star Corporation charges that Smith's action was prompted by the desire to deprive it of its rightful interest in the property and that all these steps were taken in collusion with the plaintiff.

After the corporation had received the assignment of the property, it promptly applied in Special Term of the Supreme Court to be substituted as a party defendant in place of the defendant, Albert Smith. Special Term did not pass upon the merits of the application but denied the motion solely on the grounds that the issues involved were already on appeal before this court; The corporation thereupon made a motion to be substituted in place of Albert Smith before this court on the argument of this appeal. This court has examined the assignment to the corporation and finds said assignment to be legal and binding, $\underset{X}{\overset{3}{}}$ Under that assignment, the corporation is sub-rogated to all the rights held by Albert Smith. This court further rules that Albert Smith had no right to take further action in the litigation after assigning his interest in the property to the White Star Corporation. His attempt to withdraw his answer, to consent to entry of judgment and to abandon his appeal are all Ineffectual. The White Star Corporation is entitled to be substituted as a party in interest in place of Albert Smith and its motion for such relief is therefore granted. All papers hereafter submitted should indicate that the corporation is the true party whose present interest is adverse to that of the plaintiff, George Jones.

This court is now prepared to consider the merits of the appeal. The present defendant argues that triable issues are involved and that summary judgment in favor of the plaintiff should not have been granted. In his answer in Supreme Court, the original defendant pleaded the defense of the Statute of Limitations. The court properly disposed of that

[4] defense by reference to the mortgage moratorium statute. That statute prohibits the bringing of foreclosure suit where the debor had defaulted in reducing only the principal of the debt. In the case at bar, the defendant Albert Smith was not in arrears in payment of interest on the mortgage debt but only in reduction of the face amount of the debt.

The substantive issues of the case are therefore open for our consideration. Albert Smith never contended that the bond and mortgage were not legal and binding instruments when made. His main defense to the action was that the principal sum due had been reduced to less than one-third of the original amount, partly by payment and partly by forgiveness of certain installments. The Supreme Court rejected both of these defenses on the grounds that the defendant had failed to produce any substantial evidence in favor of his contentions. However, as the present appellant contends that credible evidence as to certain payments does exist, we direct that a trial of those issues be held. [5]

EXAMINATION SECTION
TEST 1

OFFICIAL DICTATION
1st CASE
(175 Words Per Minute For Five (5) Minutes)

The Fulton Savings Bank was the owner of two separate mortgages, each in the principal sum of fourteen thousand five hundred dollars, which were liens on two separate premises near the intersection of Broadway and 42nd Street in the Borough of Manhattan. The principal sums were due on these mortgages on January tenth, nineteen eighty-eight. The record indicates that six years later, Edward Thomas, the mortgagor, was in default for taxes, water, and interest in the amount of fourteen hundred ninety-eight dollars and fifty cents.

The principal sum of fourteen thousand five hundred dollars due on each of these mortgages, according to their terms, on January tenth, nineteen eighty-eight, was also unpaid.

In order to insure preservation of the property, Edward Thomas, the owner of the premises, executed and delivered an assignment of rents in which an agent was appointed to manage the premises and apply the rents and profits of said premises for disbursements for the ordinary and proper maintenance and upkeep of the mortgaged premises. The instrument also irrevocably $\overset{1}{x}$ assigned to the mortgagee, the Fulton Savings Bank, all sums received by the owner from the aforementioned agent to be applied in its direction and in any order it might determine, on account of the arrears of taxes, water rates, assessments, fire insurance premiums, premiums on liability policies, interest, and installments of principal. It further provided that the aforesaid agency should continue and the powers of the said agent should remain in full force and effect until all arrears of taxes and other charges, which might be liens upon said mortgaged premises in priority to the above-mentioned mortgage, and all arrears of principal and interest upon said mortgage debt had been fully paid.

This arrangement still continues in force and effect, never having been rescinded or modified, and as of the present date, the record indicates that the principal of each mortgage has been reduced to ten thousand eight hundred dollars with interest of six percent from said date. All other obligations are paid.

Recently, John Alexander, owner of mortgages on these premises, $\overset{2}{x}$ junior in priority to the mortgages above referred to, commenced an action to foreclose his mortgages, and in that action a receiver of the rents was duly appointed by an ex parte order of this court. The receiver immediately investigated the situation. Said receiver, informed of the foregoing assignment, has now moved this court for an order restraining the Fulton Savings Bank and its agents from interfering with him in the collection of the rents, and directing said bank and its agents to turn over to him any of the rents they may have collected from time of his appointment as receiver herein.

By a separate motion, the Fulton Savings Bank and its agent have moved to vacate the order appointing the receiver in the action to foreclose the junior mortgages. The bank contends that by virtue of the assignment above described, it is entitled to apply the net rentals accruing from the premises on account of the principal as well as the interest secured by its aforesaid mortgages until the same shall have $\overset{3}{x}$ been paid.

The attorney representing the plaintiff in the motion to foreclose the junior mortgages has submitted an affidavit in support of the receiver's motion and in opposition to that made by the Bank. He contends that a reading of the assignment in question indicates the intention of the parties to terminate the assignment when all of the arrears which existed at the time the assignment was executed have been paid and not, as contended by the Bank, when the principals of the mortgages have been fully paid. Plaintiff further contends that the net income from premises is in excess of the three percent statutory amortization to which the first mortgagee is entitled under the present moratory statutes, that said first mortgagee is not entitled to be paid any additional sums on account of principal beyond three percent, and that to hold otherwise would unjustly deprive the second mortgagee of his legal rights under the junior mortgages covering the premises in question.

Whatever view one might take of the first contention set forth $\overset{4}{x}$ in the preceding paragraph as urged by the attorney for the junior mortgagee, the result of the present applications must be the same. When the foregoing assignments of rents were executed, the so-called *moratory statutes* were in force. Under the provisions of Section ten seventy-seven a of the Civil Practice Act, effective August twenty-sixth, nineteen fifty-three, the right to foreclose a mortgage by reason of the non-payment of past due water taxes, other taxes, and interest was not disturbed.

Prior to the enactment of the moratory statutes, a different rule would have applied. Indeed, had the assignment of rents in this case been executed prior to the enactment of the moratory statutes, the bank's rights thereunder could not thereafter have been disturbed as they were vested property and contract rights. In this case, however, the assignment was executed and delivered on March twenty-seventh, nineteen fifty-four, after the moratory statute, Section ten seventy-seven, a and c of the Civil Practice Act, became effective. Thus the statute does apply. $\overset{5}{x}$

OFFICIAL DICTATION
2nd CASE
(175 Words Per Minute For Five (5) Minutes)

The record before us indicates that the Lehigh Valley National Bank and Trust Company deeded to the Lakeside Corporation, a parcel of land, used as a children's camp, on Silver Lake in Essex County. The deed was recorded September 24, 1987, Upon the execution and delivery of the deed, the Lakeside Corporation gave the bank a first mortgage on the property in the total sum of twenty-one thousand dollars. This mortgage was actually recorded in the Essex County Clerk's office shortly after its delivery.

A few weeks thereafter the Lakeside Corporation gave a second mortgage on the same premises to the plaintiff and to the defendant Jones to secure the payment of the sum of eighty-five hundred dollars. The plaintiff and the defendant Jones each owned a one-half interest in the second mortgage. This mortgage was not acknowledged or recorded until nearly five years had elapsed. It covered not only the real estate but all the fixtures, articles of personal property, equipment, and other furnishings in the buildings on $\overset{1}{x}$ the premises, or then or thereafter attached to or used in connection with the premises. It also provided that should the lien of the mortgage be held inferior to the lien of a conditional sale contract or chattel mortgage covering any of the personal property, then, in the event of default, all interest of the mortgagor in such personal property was assigned to the mortgagee together with the credit for any payments made thereon by the mortgagor.

By deed dated June fifteenth, nineteen ninety-two, and recorded six or seven months later, the Lakeside Corporation conveyed the premises to Frank Albert, a relative of defendant Jones. Two judgments were secured against the Lakeside Corporation. One judgment in favor of the State Industrial Commission for fourteen hundred twenty-eight dollars and thirty-three cents was docketed within a few days and another in favor of Mason and Company for seven hundred and thirteen dollars and eighty cents was docketed on September third, nineteen ninety-two.

Shortly thereafter, as the record indicates, Frank Albert leased the property $\overset{2}{x}$ to defendant George J. Robinson for a term expiring on September thirtieth, nineteen ninety-seven. The lease included use of the real property, buildings, and equipment then on the premises, or stored elsewhere, except for certain specified articles. In addition to the annual rent payable under the lease, there was an agreement by Robinson to employ Frank Jones, husband of defendant, Ethel Jones, as camp superintendent and purchasing agent, at a specified salary. There was also a provision for the payment of a certain amount for various expenses which included interest on the mortgages, insurance, and taxes. The lease also provided that an inventory of equipment owned by the lessor and the lessee should be taken and that such equipment should remain their personal property. All buildings and other structures erected upon the premises became the property of the lessor but the cost of all equipment purchased was to be adjusted between the parties.

The record further indicates that plaintiff instituted an action to foreclose the second mortgage. A supplemental summons and an amended complaint $\overset{3}{x}$ in that action were served on defendant Robinson on August twenty-fifth, nineteen ninety-two. Jones, one of the owners of the mortgage, refused to become a plaintiff and was made a defendant in that action. Defendant Robinson appeared in the action and served an answer to the amended complaint in which he denied on information and belief the material allegations thereof. In addition to that, he alleged six separate and distinct defenses.

The first defense pleaded the six-year statute of limitations.

As the second defense, Robinson alleged that the lease had been given to him by defendant Jones, by authority of and for the benefit of plaintiff. He further alleged that under the terms of the lease, plaintiff and defendant Jones had covenanted that Robinson should quietly enjoy the premises and hence that the plaintiff was estopped from asserting any claim against Robinson.

The third defense alleged Robinson had placed certain buildings, fixtures, and chattels on the premises, for use in the operation of the camp, which were not covered by the mortgages^4_x and that these structures could be removed without substantial injury to the freehold.

As the fourth defense, Robinson alleged that plaintiff had ratified the lease and thereby acknowledged the right of Robinson to remove the property.

The fifth defense stated that the mortgage was void for want of consideration.

For a sixth defense and counterclaim against the plaintiff and defendant Jones, Robinson alleged that Jones and Albert had agreed in the lease to pay off the mortgage and that foreclosure thereof would damage him in the sum of twenty-five thousand dollars. Robinson demanded that the complaint be dismissed and that he have judgment against the defendants Jones and Albert for the damages that he would sustain.

Defendants Jones and Albert served replies denying the material allegations of the defenses and the counterclaim and asked for judgment dismissing them. Plaintiff moved to strike out the first, fourth, and fifth defenses contained in the answer on the ground that the defenses were insufficient in law. By these motions plaintiff is attempting to obtain decision before trial.^5_x

TEST 2

OFFICIAL DICTATION
OPENING
(175 Words Per Minute - 3 Minutes)

Mr. Cohen's question is rather broad. If he intended to inquire solely as to the effect of failure to give notice under the circumstances stated, the answer, I think, is simple. The principle is well established that the provisions of section 44 of the Personal Property Law must be strictly construed (Mott v. Reeves, 125 Misc., 511, aff'd 213 App. Div., 718, aff'd 246 N.Y., 567). The section is barren of any requirement, or even a suggestion of requirement, that the purchaser make an independent search for creditors. The Bulk Sales Law requires that those creditors must be notified whose names and addresses are stated in the list furnished by the seller or of whom the purchaser has knowledge. That does not mean possible creditors, but known creditors. There is no basis for reading into the statute that which is not explicitly stated therein, nor which may not be $\underset{x}{^1}$ fairly implied therefrom. It seems clear that under the circumstances stated by Mr. Cohen the purchaser may proceed with complete assurance against liability to creditors if any later appear. Must the purchaser, however, against the possibility of undisclosed creditors, make and keep the inventory called for? Caution requires an affirriative reply in the absence of adjudication on this point.

Many lawyers have deemed it sufficient to take the affidavit of the seller and to withhold from the purchase price a sum sufficient to pay the creditors disclosed to the purchaser, without complying with the other provisions of the statute relating to inventory and notice. Under such circumstances, would not a creditor, undisclosed and unknown to the purchaser, properly seek to impose liability on the purchaser because each requirement of the statute had not been complied with? The question does not appear to have been presented to the courts.

Another troublesome $\underset{x}{^2}$ point concerns the making of the inventory by the seller. What is reasonable diligence in ascertaining the cost price to the seller of each article included in the sale (and there may be thousands of similar articles purchased at various tines, the original cost of which can be traced, if at all, only with the greatest difficulty), and how the purchaser (who must pay the penalty) can effectively control the diligence of the seller is perplexing indeed to the lawyer who must advise the purchaser in the transaction.

Annoying, too, is the requirement that the notice to creditors must be *of the proposed sale and of the price, terms, and conditions thereof.* There may be a lengthy contract, with multitudinous terms, each of which is an integral part of the contract, but in most of which the creditor can have no legitimate interest. Nevertheless a precise compliance with the terms x of the statute would require the placing of the entire contract in the hands of every creditor, large or small.

EXAMINATION SECTION
TESTIMONY

(175 Words per minute - 5 minutes)

Cross examination by defendant's counsel:

QUESTION:	Do you remember the month that the man from the City saw you in this case?
ANSWER:	I remember it very well.
QUESTION:	What month was that?
ANSWER:	That was the day before Thanksgiving.
QUESTION:	He wrote down what you told him, at that time, did he not?
ANSWER:	I do not know what he did.
QUESTION:	You were there. Did you not see him?
ANSWER:	I was there. Sure I saw him.
QUESTION:	I ask you this question: What he wrote down was what you told him?

> Plaintiff's Counsel: I object. The witness is not competent to testify to that.
> The Court: No, unless he read it.

QUESTION:	Did he not write down what you told him?
ANSWER:	I do not know what he did.
QUESTION:	Did he not read something to you?
ANSWER:	No. He was propounding questions to me.
QUESTION:	Do you say that he did not read you, the statement he made?
ANSWER:	No, I did not give him any. And the doctors did not give him any. He wanted them both to give him statements.
QUESTION:	Did the man tell you from what department of the City of ^1_X New York he was?
ANSWER:	Yes.
QUESTION:	What department?
ANSWER:	The Corporation Counsel's office.
QUESTION:	Or was it the Department of Finance, or the Comptroller's office?
ANSWER:	No, he said he was from the Corporation Counsel's office.
QUESTION:	What was his name? Do you remember his name?
ANSWER:	No. He did not introduce himself.
QUESTION:	Do you remember telling the man from the City that you did not know the number of the house in front of which Doctor MacDonald fell?
ANSWER:	I know, if I told him anything, it was ---

QUESTION: You did not tell him anything?

ANSWER: No, and there is no witness to corroborate it. He wanted me to sign a paper, and he wanted the doctors to sign a paper. He was the means of having me fired out of the hospital, 1 was there through courtesy, not because I was mentally disabled.

> Defendant's Counsel: Will you please keep still? I ask that all the answer be striken out.
> The Court: Strike it out.

QUESTION: Did he want you to sign a paper?

ANSWER: Yes.

QUESTION: These are the papers he wanted you to sign; is that correct?

ANSWER: I do ^2_X not know. I did not look at them. I did not rise. He sat in a chair. I was sitting farther than the table away from him.

QUESTION: Did you sign anything?

> Plaintiff's counsel: He stated he did not see it.

ANSWER: I never signed anything.

QUESTION: And, after you told this man from the Corporation Counsel's office or from the City of New York this story, he wrote it down and read the statement to you?

ANSWER: He did not get any story from me. He asked Doctor Schatz if he would be a witness to the fact. I told him I would sign nothing. And Doctor Schatz told him he would sign nothing either.

QUESTION: I am not asking you anything that Doctor Schatz told. I am talking about you, only.

ANSWER: That is what happened there. I did not want to be botheredwith it.

QUESTION: Did he not read this all over to you, and did you not say that it was correct in all respects?

ANSWER: No, I never gave the man a statement.

> Defendant's Counsel: That is all.
> Plaintiff's Counsel: May I have ^3_X the privilege of a few questions, your Honor?
> The Court: Proceed.

Re-direct Examination by Plaintiff's Counsel:

QUESTION: I hand you Plaintiff's Exhibit 5 and ask you to look at it carefully, also Defendant's Exhibit B. Do you observe, from these two exhibits, that there are five sections of the ventilation grating?

3 (#1)

ANSWER:	Yes.
QUESTION:	In front of 711 and 715 Replogle Avenue?
ANSWER:	Yes.
QUESTION:	And the five sections are both shown in these two exhibits, are they?
ANSWER:	Yes.
QUESTION:	Do you observe also, that each of those five sections is again subdivided into four parts?
ANSWER:	Yes, sir.
QUESTION:	Four parts in.width?
ANSWER:	Yes, sir.
QUESTION:	Now, when you testified on cross examination that, so far as you remember, the pegs were only in front of the section where the Reverend Mackler fell ---
ANSWER:	Yes.
QUESTION:	Did you or did you not mean, or tell me what you meant. Did you mean that the pegs were entirely across the four subdivisions of the southern section?
ANSWER:	Yes.

> Defendant's Counsel: Now, wait, please. If your Honor please, I object to this, on the ground that I asked the question and your Honor asked the question, and $\underset{X}{4}$ I asked the witness if he understood your Honor's question.
> The Court: Yes, but he answered both ways across. I am going to let him straighten it out.

QUESTION:	In referring to this grating here, let us be sure we understand our terminology. I am going to call these five different parts five sections, and each of these five sections in turn has four parts.
ANSWER:	Yes.
QUESTION:	Now, counsel, up to this time, called each of those four p.arts sections; but let us forget that terminology a minute. Were there pegs all the way across the southern end of the southern section, which included four parts?
ANSWER:	I believe they were.

Re-cross Examination by Defendant's Counsel:

QUESTION:	I asked you -- pointed out on this photograph that I held in front of the jury--- I have this up, and I asked you whether the pegs ran across from one side to the other, and you said no, did you not?
ANSWER:	Well, because I looked through two pairs of glasses, and it looked the same.
QUESTION:	You saw the picture up there, and I asked you to look at $\underset{X}{5}$ it.

4 (#1)

Direct Examination by Plaintiff's Counsel:

QUESTION: Do you know the plaintiff in this case?

ANSWER: I do.

QUESTION: Did you see the plaintiff in this case on December 22?

ANSWER: I did.

QUESTION: Will you tell the Court and jury under what circumstances you saw him and describe for the court and jury also what you saw about him?

ANSWER: Well, the doorbell rang. I went upstairs and answered it. A gentleman stood there with a bloody handkerchief to his mouth, and he asked whether he could see the doctor. He was very much shaken and agitated, and, in fact, he was trembling. And I said I was afraid he could not see the doctor, because he was ill.

> Defendant's Counsel: I beg your pardon. I am sorry to interrupt, but we cannot have anything like that.
> The Court: You cannot have any conversation. How was the doctor? Was he ill?

QUESTION: Just describe what you saw yourself about the Reverend MacDonald.

ANSWER: He stood there with his handkerchief to his face. His handkerchief was bloody, and he was pale. In fact, he was livid.

> Plaintiff's Counsel: A little louder. I cannot hear you.
> The Witness: He was livid.

QUESTION: By that do you mean his face was white?

ANSWER: No. Livid is something more than white. Livid is a sort of blue white. It is worse than pale, if you ever saw it.

QUESTION: What else did you notice about Doctor Mackler?

ANSWER: Well, I noticed that he was trembling. In fact, he was shaking so much that I was---well, just a little bit nervous.

QUESTION: Was the doctor ill that day?

ANSWER: Yes, he was; but he was not in bed.

> Plaintiff's Counsel: That is all.

Cross Examination by Defendant's Counsel:

QUESTION: Mr. Gorman, was the doctor out on Sunday, last Sunday? ANSWER: Last Sunday, I do not know. He was out one day to get a newspaper; but I do not know whether it was Saturday or Sunday.

QUESTION: Was he out on Sunday?

ANSWER: Let's see. I cannot answer that. I do not know whether he was or not. I was not home most of the day.

5 (#1)

The Court: Next question.

QUESTION: Do you know whether any subpoena has been served on the doctor personally to come to court?

ANSWER: Not to my knowledge.

> Defendant's Counsel: That is all.
> Plaintiff's Counsel: May I ask one other question, your Honor?
> The Court: Yes.

Re-direct Examination by Plaintiff's Counsel:

QUESTION: Did you recognize Doctor Mackler when you first saw him that day?

ANSWER: No, I did not.

QUESTION: You say he had the handkerchief over his mouth this way?

ANSWER: Yes.

QUESTION: How long had you known him, Mr. Gorman?

ANSWER: That is a little hard to answer; but I should say over a period of—well, I could not answer that--I could answer it, perhaps, in another way.

QUESTION: Can you tell us about how long a time? That is all.

ANSWER: I am not very much---possibly, over a period of ten years.

QUESTION: You say that, when he came over there, his handkerchief was over his mouth that way?

ANSWER: Yes.

QUESTION: You did not recognize him?

ANSWER: I did not recognize him.

Re-cross Examination by Defendant's Counsel:

QUESTION: Was there not anything about his dress that indicated that it was Doctor Mackler?

ANSWER: Why, yes, he had his regular clerical garb on, as far as I can remember.

QUESTION: How long was he talking to you, Mr Gorman?

ANSWER: Not very long.

QUESTION: Would you say ten minutes?

ANSWER: No, not as long as that.

QUESTION: Five minutes?

ANSWER: Oh, yes, I think so.

QUESTION: Then he went inside?

ANSWER: Well, yes. If you would just let me tell it in my own way, perhaps that would be better.

QUESTION:	You talked to him perhaps five minutes before the door there?
ANSWER:	Yes.
QUESTION:	And he went in the house. How long did he stay in the house?
ANSWER:	Well, that is a little difficult to say.
QUESTION:	Did you see him leave the house?
ANSWER:	No, I did not.

THE COURT'S CHARGE TO THE JURY

Gentlemen of the jury, it is my custom in charging a jury to stand as counsel have been standing in summing up to you and as counsel rises when it addresses the court, because you gentlemen are now the court. The entire burden and duty in this case now rests on your shoulders. My part of this case has been comparatively small. I had very few technical questions of evidence to rule upon. There were days that passed when I believe there was not a single question raised on questions of evidence. My sole duty is to sit here and keep order and listen to the testimony so that I may properly charge you at the close of this case.

The law involved in this case is quite simple. It is just as simple as might be involved in a contract for building a garage in your backyard. It is, of course, an important case, and the weightiest duty in this case falls on your shoulders. You are the sole judges of the fact. You must determine where the truth in this case lies after I have charged you.

This case drawn out for some days, but I assure you, gentlemen, that it might have been much longer but for the very able work of counsel for both the plaintiff and the defendant in this case, and I wish to compliment them on the way the cases of their clients were presented. I have had cases of this nature before and I might say that never have I heard a case so well presented on either side. I wish also to compliment you gentlemen on your close attention. I realize that it has been a great sacrifice to many of you to be with us for so long. Some of you told me that you were making business sacrifices, but you come to an end of your labors now, or will shortly, and I want to compliment you on the close attention that you have paid to the testimony.

Counsel have very fully summed up their cases. I did not impose any stringent limit on their summation and I feel that the facts are fresh in your minds. It will, of course, be necessary for me to refer from time to time to some of the facts in this case to point the rules of law which I shall give to you. It is necessary in each case to lay before the jury those general principles of law which apply to all cases in a civil court.

In all actions in this court, gentlemen, the law places upon the plaintiff the burden of proving and convincing the jury by a fair preponderance of the credible evidence in the case that he or it is entitled to the verdict it seeks. When we refer to the fair preponderance of the credible evidence we do not mean that the plaintiff must bring in the greater number of witnesses or that it must offer the greater number of exhibits into evidence. We refer entirely to the quality of the testimony of the witnesses, and the quality of the exhibits, and the weight that the exhibits as offered by the parties to the action may have. The mere bringing of an action does not mean, of course, that the plaintiff must recover. You must feel, after having listened to all the testimony, that the plaintiff has convinced you that its version of the case is the correct and proper and truthful version of the case, and that applying the law as I give it to you, the plaintiff is entitled to the verdict that it seeks.

In weighing the testimony you will, of course, take into consideration the character of the testimony of the various witnesses; their interest in the case and, of course, the manner in which they have testified; their qualifications in the event of their testifying as experts; their education, their experience, and all those things which you believe have a bearing on the quality of the testimony and the weight which you believe should be given to it. Take the testimony of all of the witnesses. Take into consideration the facts as they were brought before you by the exhibits.in the case. From that determine where the truth in this case lies; whether or not the plaintiff has sustained the burden of proof to which we have referred. If, after considering all the evidence in the case, you are unable to determine where the truth in this case lies, then the plaintiff has failed to sustain the burden of proof and you must find for the defendant.

Plaintiff alleges that through the. fault of the defendant City of New York the contract which it undertook to execute was not finished within the contract time; that because of its inability to finish in contract time due, it says, to the fault and breach on the part of the City of New York in fulfillment of its covenants that it was damaged due to the fact that after the close of the contract period it was obliged to pay increased prices for both labor and material and that the prolonged use of capital was another item of damage.

EXAMINATION SECTION
TESTIMONY

OFFICIAL DICTATION
PART I

(175 Words per minute for three (3) minutes)

We address ourselves at the outset to the question of whether or not there was an investment of the funds of the aforementioned estate in the mortgages in question. The trial court held that there was an investment, whereas the Appellate Division held that there was not. In our statement of the facts we have outlined the details with reference to the disposition of the funds of the said estate after the moneys were deposited with the City Officer, with particular reference to that portion of the moneys belonging to a certain firm of attorneys. The City Officer's records and the testimony of one witness show clearly that the funds deposited in the said estate were actually used to pay off moneys due to certain accounts and that the shares in two mortgages, formerly allocated to these accounts, were allocated on the books of the City Officer to the said $\frac{1}{x}$ estate.

This transaction, in our view, amounted to investments of the funds of the said estate in the two mortgages and the trial court so found. The defendants urge, however, that the allocations made by the City Officer were mere bookkeeping entries and not, therefore, investments of the estate funds. However, the practice followed with reference to the said estate was typical of that employed with respect to many other accounts and has frequently been held to constitute an investment. One court said that the money was paid to the City Officer and was immediately deposited by him to the credit of his account in a designated bank. It apparently remained there on deposit for a few days when it was invested in a manner evidently common in his office, but which is not criticized by the parties interested in the fund.

The City Officer held a mortgage which covered $\frac{2}{x}$ certain vacant lots in the City of New York.

He was later ordered to pay over certain moneys to the persons entitled, and desiring to keep this mortgage and certain others in which those moneys had been invested, he used the moneys deposited, in this case, to make the payments required. The balance of the fund was thereupon deposited in the trust company where it remained until the following year, when it was invested in a similar manner, and by the same process, in certain other mortgages held by the City Officer.

Another Court in a similar case referred to this practice of the City Officer, several times in the course of its opinion and always spoke of the transaction as an investment. It had been customary for the City Officer to make payment in cash of amounts which had been invested by transferring the investment to any desired fund. $\frac{3}{x}$

2 (#1)

PART II
(Testimony of 175 words per minute for 5 minutes by 4 voices)

P.Q. Now, suppose we clear up the matter about what attention you received after your accident. You say you were first picked up on a stretcher and taken to the nearest hospital emergency ward. Is that right, and was anything done for you there?

W.A. I think I was kept there about an hour while they were calling up an ambulance. They didn't try to do anything for me there, although my hip was paining me badly. I believe they didn't have any accommodations at that hospital for people with injured legs. It was a mistake to take me there in the first place.

P.Q. In other words, you were there about an hour and nothing was done for you. You were just lying out on the stretcher for all that time, and you said your left hip kept paining you ---

D. I object to this line of questioning. Let him ask one thing at a time.

J. They are simple questions as to what the situation was. Continue.

P.Q. Your left hip kept paining you, and later on they had $\underset{x}{\overset{1}{=}}$ occasion to bring the ambulance, is that right?

W.A. Yes, it was paining me, of course, and after the ambulance came they took me down town to the hospital and put me into the emergency ward, and they called up my doctor.

P.Q. That was about two and a half hours after the accident occurred, and while you were in the emergency ward, was anything done for you while you were waiting for your doctor to arrive?

W.A. Well, I was in agony all the time, but nothing happened till my doctor came and he had me put on a bed, and he rigged the bed up in such a way that a pulley could be put on to keep my leg stretched.

P.A. How long did you remain in bed with this pulley contraption attached to your leg, and what other things were done for you?

W.A. Oh, I was in bed for three or for days with the pulley on, and they took x-ray pictures with the machine right there while I was in bed, and nest thing, $\underset{x}{\overset{2}{=}}$ they took me into the operating room and gave me ether. I was under that ether for three or four hours, and when I woke up, they had a cast from my toes to my armpit.

P.Q. Before you went under the ether and during the five or six days that you were lying with this pulley on your left foot, did the left leg or the left hip hurt you?

W.A.   Oh, yes, it hurt me all the time both before and after the cast was put on and I was so bad that they gave me needles. They gave me needles for about four weeks, till the doctor said they could not give me any more and that I would have to do without it. I never slept a wink from when I went in there until I got out, except in the day time, I might doze off for a few minutes, that is all. And I asked the doctor couldn't he do anything for me---

J.   I think we should not have any conversations. $\frac{3}{x}$ He must not tell us what the doctor said to him. Just let him tell how he felt himself.

D.   Yes, and I object to this line of testimony as purely speculative and further, on the ground that it is not on the proper basis. Let the witness be told to answer directly. The rest is incompetent, irrelevant and immaterial.

J.   Let him proceed.

P.Q.   How long was this plaster cast on you and how did you feel? Were you lying on your back? When did they finally take it off?

W.A.   The plaster cast was on me about ten weeks, and by that time I was all in, my back cut, and I was sore all over. I lost about 40 pounds and I was perspiring all the time I was in the cast. Then they cut off the top part of the cast and let a little air in, but I had to lie on my back on the other., half for another two or three weeks. It must have been over three months before they measured $\frac{4}{x}$ me for a brace and gave me crutches. The first day I got up, I could only sit up for an hour, but every day they put me in a wheel chair for a little longer and at last I took a change with the crutches and the brace, and I could just navigate.

P.Q.   You had some expenses while in the hospital, didn't you? And did you pay these bills week by week as they became due?

W.A.   Yes, and I have all receipts here. ---

J.   What is the total amount? Instead of offering all the separate receipts in evidence, just add them up and tell us the amount.

D.   We will concede the amount is a fair and reasonable charge.

J.   Why don't you say what the amount is and they will concede it. Let your assistant add up the amount and they will concede, that is what he had paid.

P.Q.   Now, you had bills for the doctor, for braces and crutches and even for the ambulance. Didn't you?

4 (#1)

W.A.   Yes, I paid about a thousand dollars. $\frac{5}{x}$

PART III
(Testimony for 4 minutes by four voices)

P.Q.   Now, doctor, you may refresh your recollection from this record as far as-you can. Did you see the plaintiff soon after he came to the hospital, and will you describe his condition at the time you saw him to the Court and Jury? ---

       J.   Doctor, you can look at that record to refresh your recollection, but the hospital record is what they call hearsay evidence. It might be made up by anybody. The best evidence is the testimony of you yourself, but if you should forget anything, you may look through that to refresh your memory, but do not read from it.

W.A.   I saw him the day he was admitted, and he was complaining of pain in the region of his left hip. The left leg was pulled out from the body, the left foot turned out from the body, and he was unable to lift the left leg from the bed. There was pain when we tried to move the leg in the region of the left hip and abnormal mobility which made me think that he had a fracture.

P.Q.   If you recall, what did you do for him at that time and later on, when you took charge $\frac{1}{x}$ of developments?

W.A,   We had x-rays taken shortly after his admission and then he was put in a form of traction with pulleys and. weights extending to his leg to try and pull it down into position. At the end of two or three days the leg was pulled down sufficiently and then I took him to the operating room and under an anaesthetic, I applied the plaster of Paris cast.

P.Q.   How many x-ray pictures did you have taken altogether, and what facts did they show?

W.A,   Ten pictures altogether. They showed the fracture, and from time to time, the progress of the healing, and they indicated what were the next steps to be taken. On the basis of these x-rays, we know how to apply the cast, we can see how the fracture is healing, the new bone forming, and then we can judge when it is time to remove part or all of the cast.

P.Q.   Will you describe generally his condition at the time he left the hospital, and what you believe to be his present condition.

W.A.   Well, he left the hospital wearing a splint which did not allow any weight bearing on the left leg itself, but allowed him to $\frac{2}{x}$ walk. After wearing this for three months we commenced to let him bear weight on his leg. When I examined him last week his left leg appeared to be about an inch shorter than his right leg. It can move fairly easily in and out, though the muscles in that leg differ in size from those in the right leg. The condition is permanent, I would say.

P.Q. Supposing, doctor, that a man of fifty-four years of age was walking along a sidewalk on which snow and ice has been packed down---

J. I think we could save the time of the Court and Jury by stating, without putting any hypothetical question, that such a fall could precipitate the injuries described by the doctor.

D. I will join that concession, except that I would like the doctor to state that he considered that a good union or repair resulted, if that is so.

W.A. Well, callous had formed and nature had produced a good union, although the fractured portion was a little thicker than the other side. For a man of his age I think he got a very good result, but of course there was some shortening and loss of flexibility. $\frac{3}{x}$

PART IV
(Charge of 175 words per minute for 5 minutes by the Judge)

Ladies and gentlemen of the jury, this action is brought by the plaintiff to recover damages for personal injuries which he alleges he sustained by reason of the negligence of these defendants. The plaintiff maintains that while he was walking on the southerly sidewalk, before referred to, he slipped and fell to the ground as a result of which he sustained the injuries which you have heard descibed. The plaintiff contends that the City of New York negligently permitted snow and ice to accumulate and remain upon the sidewalk, rendering passage on the sidewalk dangerous to persons walking upon it.

The plaintiff further contends that the defendant was also careless and negligent in that during the course of his business he permitted water to be discharged from his premises, flow upon the sidewalk in winter weather and freeze, thus creating a dangerous and unsafe condition. The plaintiff further claims that the condition of the sidewalk such as you have heard described existed for some

time prior to the accident and that the defendants had notice $\frac{1}{x}$ of the defective condition and should have remedied it. The defendants deny any and all responsibility for the accident. They contend that the sidewalk under the existing conditions and circumstances was maintained in a safe manner, and that the accident was caused not by any omission on their part but by the carelessness of the plaintiff himself. The defendant denies that he permitted water to be discharged from his premises and freeze upon the sidewalk and insists that he took all the proper precautions that might reasonably be expected of him in the maintenance of his premises. Both he and the City contend that at the time of the accident and prior thereto the winter weather was such that they did all that was humanly possible and that, therefore, they were in no manner careless or negligent.

Now, except as I have stated here, I feel I cannot aid you by a discussion of the evidence. The testimony of the several witnesses is fresh in your minds and your recollection is as good, if not [2] better than mine. The case has been tried by experienced and able counsel on both sides and if I should pick out portions of the testimony for discussion I might unconsciously lead you to suppose that I considered important matters which you considered unimportant and vice versa. So as to the facts, *I* am going to leave the case entirely with you, leaving it to you to discuss the testimony wholly uninfluenced by anything that *I* say to you concerning it.

Now, this is a negligence action. Negligence may be defined as the failure or the omission to do some act or perform some duty which one person owes to another. More simply defined, it is the absence of such care as a reasonably prudent person would be expected to use under the circumstances. Before the plaintiff can recover, the law places on him the burden of proving to your satisfaction by a fair preponderance of the credible evidence that he was injured by reason of the negligence of these defendants. He must prove that [3] the accident was caused solely and wholly by the negligence of the defendants or either of them, and if he fails in that, then no matter how much you may sympathize with the misfortune that has overtaken him, he may not in justice recover damages and your verdict must be for the defendants.

The plaintiff must also prove that this accident in which it is claimed he was injured was not brought about or contributed to by any negligence, however slight on his part, for if you find that the plaintiff was guilty of contributory negligence, even in the slightest degree, he cannot recover against these defendants. The fact that an accident happened and that the plaintiff was injured are not in themselves reasons sufficient for you to determine that the plaintiff must recover, for there is no presumption of negligence to be drawn from the mere happening of an accident. A further burden resting upon the plaintiff is to prove that the accident in which it is claimed that he was injured was a [4] competent producing cause of the injuries claimed to have been sustained and for the condition it is claimed the plaintiff is now suffering from.

I charge you, ladies and gentlemen, that the defendants are not insurers of the safety of pedestrians. The City of New York is not expected to maintain its streets and roads, in such an absolutely perfect condition as to render accidents impossible. It is expected to use reasonable care and prudence in detecting and remedying any defect which might be anticipated as dangerous and liable to cause an accident. The measure of its duty in this respect is reasonable care.

Actual notice means what it says. By constructive notice is meant that a condition has existed for a sufficient length of time as to charge one with presumptive knowledge of that condition. It is for you to say whether the time that this condition existed, if at all, was sufficiently long enough to charge the City with constructive notice.

Now, I thank you all for your attention. Are there any questions? [5]

PRACTICE AND DRILL IN SHORTHAND OUTLINES

FOR

LEGAL (HEARING/REPORTING) STENOGRAPHERS

(SIMPLIFIED & ANNIVERSARY)

CONTENTS

	Page
A Fortiori ...... Adjudication	1
Advance ...... Appropriation	2
Appurtenant ...... Bench	3
Beneficiary ...... Certiorari	4
Charge ...... Consignee	5
Consignor ...... Criteria (pl.)	6
Damages ...... Deterioration	7
Detriment ...... Duress	8
Easement ...... Evidence	9
Ex Contractu ...... Fiscal	10
Foreclosure (Sale) ...... Guilty	11
Habeas Corpus ...... Indemnify	12
Indemnity ...... Issue	13
Jeopardy ...... Libel	14
Lien ...... Mortgage	15
Mortgagee ...... Nunc Pro Tunc	16
Object ...... Ordinance	17
Parol ...... Preponderance	18
Prima Facie ...... Punitive	19
Quash ...... Remand	20
Replevin ...... Situs	21
Sovereign ...... Syllabus	22
Tenant ...... Unilateral	23
Vacate ...... Writ	24

PRACTICE AND DRILL IN SHORTHAND OUTLINES

FOR

LEGAL STENOGRAPHERS

(SIMPLIFIED & ANNIVERSARY)

	SIMPLIFIED	ANNIVERSARY	
a fortiori			A term meaning you can reason one thing from the existence of certain facts.
a priori			From what goes before.
ab initio			From the beginning.
abate			To diminish or put an end to.
abet			To encourage the commission of a crime.
abeyance			Suspension, temporary suppression.
abide			To accept the consequences of.
abrogate			To annul, repeal, or destroy.
abscond			To hide or absent oneself to avoid legal action.
abstract			A summary.
abut			To border on, to touch.
access			Approach; in real property law it means the right of the owner of property to the use of the highway or road next to his land, without obstruction by intervening property owners.
accessory			In criminal law, it means the person who contributes or aids in the commission of a crime.
accommodated party			One to whom credit is extended on the strength of another person signing a commercial paper.

	SIMPLIFIED	ANNIVERSARY	
accommodation paper			A commercial paper to which the accommodating party has put his name.
accomplice			In criminal law, it means a person who together with the principal offender commits a crime.
accord			An agreement to accept something different or less than that to which one is entitled, which extinguishes the entire obligation.
accord and satisfaction			When the agreement (accord) is executed and performed according to its terms.
account			A statement of mutual demands in the nature of debt and credit between parties.
accretion			The act of adding to a thing; in real property law, it means gradual accumulation of land by natural causes.
accrue			To grow to; to be added to.
acquiescence			A silent appearance of consent.
acquit			To legally determine the innocence of one charged with a crime.
ad infinitum			Indefinitely.
ad valorem			According to value.
addendum (sing.) addenda (pl.)			An addition; a supplement to a book.
adjudication			The judgment given in a case.

119

	SIMPLIFIED	ANNIVERSARY	
advance			In commercial law, it means to pay money or render other value before it is due.
adverse			Opposed; contrary.
advocate			(v.) To speak in favor of; (n.) one who assists, defends, or pleads for another.
affiant			A person who makes and signs an affidavit.
affidavit			A written and sworn to declaration of facts, voluntarily made.
affirm			To ratify; also when an appellate court affirms a judgment, decree, or order, it means that it is valid and right and must stand as rendered in the lower court.
aforementioned aforesaid			Before or already said.
allege			To assert.
allotment			A share or portion.
ambiguity			Uncertainty; capable of being understood in more than one way.
amendment			Any language made or proposed as a change in some principal writing.
amicus curiae			A friend of the court; one who has an interest in a case, although not a party in the case, who volunteers advice upon matters of law to the judge. For example, a brief amicus curiae.

	SIMPLIFIED	ANNIVERSARY	
amortization			To provide for a gradual extinction of (a future obligation) in advance of maturity, especially, by periodical contributions to a sinking fund which will be adequate to discharge a debt or make a replacement when it becomes necessary.
ancillary			Aiding, auxiliary.
annotation			A note added by way of comment or explanation.
answer			A written statement made by a defendant setting forth the grounds of his defense.
ante			Before.
appeal			The removal of a case from a lower court to one of superior jurisdiction for the purposes of obtaining a review.
appearance			Coming into court as a party to a suit.
appellant			The party who takes an appeal from one court or jurisdiction to another (appellate) court for review.
appellee			The party against whom an appeal is taken.
appropriate			To make a thing one's own.
appropriation			Prescribing the destination of a thing; the act of the legislature designating a particular fund, to be applied to some object of government expenditure.

	SIMPLIFIED	ANNIVERSARY	
appurtenant			Belonging to; accessory or incident to.
arbitrary			Unreasoned; not governed by any fixed rules or standard.
arguendo			By way of argument.
assent			A declaration of willingness to do something in compliance with a request.
assert			Declare.
assess			To fix the rate or amount.
assign			To transfer; to appoint; to select for a particular purpose.
assignee			One who receives an assignment.
assignor			One who makes an assignment.
averment			A positive statement of facts.

	SIMPLIFIED	ANNIVERSARY	
ball			To obtain the release of a person from legal custody by giving security and promising that he shall appear in court; to deliver (goods, etc.) in trust to a person for a special purpose.
bailment			Delivery of personal property to another to be held for a certain purpose and to be returned when the purpose is accomplished.
bailee			One to whom personal property is delivered under a contract of bailment.
bailor			The party who delivers goods to another, under a contract of bailment.
banc (or bank)			Bench; the place where a court sits permanently or regularly; also the assembly of all the judges of a court.
bankrupt			An insolvent person, technically, one declared to be bankrupt after a bankruptcy proceeding.
bar			The legal profession.
barter			A contract by which parties exchange goods for other goods.
bearer			In commercial law, it means the person in possession of a commercial paper which is payable to the bearer.
bench			The court itself; or the judge.

	SIMPLIFIED	ANNIVERSARY	
beneficiary			A person benefiting under a will, trust, or agreement.
bequest			A gift of personal property under a will.
bill			A formal written statement of complaint to a court of justice; also, a draft of an act of the legislature before it becomes a law; also, accounts for goods sold, services rendered, or work done.
bona fide			In or with good faith; honestly.
bond			An instrument by which the maker promises to pay a sum of money to another, usually providing that upon performance of a certain condition shall be void.
breach			The breaking or violating of a law, or the failure to carry out a duty.
brief			A written document, prepared by a lawyer to serve as the basis of an argument upon a case in court, usually an appellate court.
by-laws			Regulations, ordinances, or rules enacted by a corporation, association, etc., for its own government.

	SIMPLIFIED	ANNIVERSARY	
canon			A doctrine; also, a law or rule, of a church or association in particular.
caption			In a pleading, deposition or other paper connected with a case in court, it is the heading or introductory clause which shows the names of the parties, name of the court, number of the case on the docket or calendar, etc.
carrier			A person or corporation undertaking to transport persons or property.
case			A general term for an action; cause, suit, or controversy before a judicial body.
cause			A suit, litigation or action before a court.
caveat emptor			Let the buyer beware. This term expresses the rule that the purchaser of an article must examine, judge, and test it for himself, being bound to discover any obvious defects or imperfections.
certificate			A written representation that some legal formality has been complied with.
certiorari			To be informed of; the name of a writ issued by a superior court directing the lower court to send up to the former the record and proceedings of a case.

	SIMPLIFIED	ANNIVERSARY	
charge			An obligation or duty; a formal complaint; an instruction of the court to the jury upon a case.
charter			(n.) The authority by virtue of which an organized body acts; (v.) in mercantile law, it means to hire or lease a vehicle or vessel for transportation.
chattel			An article of personal property.
circuit			A division of the country, for the administration of justice; a geographical area served by a court.
citation			The act of the court by which a person is summoned or cited; also, a reference to legal authority.
civil (actions)			It indicates the private rights and remedies of individuals in contrast to the word "criminal" (actions) which relates to prosecution for violation of laws.
claim			(n.) Any demand held or asserted as of right.
codify			To arrange the laws of a country into a code.
cognizance			Notice or knowledge.
collateral			By the side; accompanying; an article or thing given to secure performance of a promise.
comity			Courtesy; the practice by which one court follows the decision of another court on the same question.

	SIMPLIFIED	ANNIVERSARY	
commit			To perform, as an act; to perpetrate, as a crime; to send a person to prison.
common law			As distinguished from law created by the enactment of legislature (called statutory law), it relates to those principles and rules of action which derive their authority solely from usages and customs of immemorial antiquity, particularly with reference to the ancient unwritten law of England. The written pronouncements of the common law are found in court decisions.
complainant			One who applies to the court for legal redress.
complaint			The pleading of a plaintiff in a civil action; or a charge that a person has committed a specified offense.
compromise			An arrangement for settling a dispute by agreement.
concur			To agree, consent.
condition			Mode or state of being; a qualification or restriction.
consign			To give in charge; commit; entrust; to send or transmit goods to a merchant, factor, or agent for sale.
consignee			One to whom a consignment is made.

	SIMPLIFIED	ANNIVERSARY	
consignor			One who sends or makes a consignment.
conspiracy			In criminal law, it means an agreement between two or more persons to commit an unlawful act.
conspirators			Persons involved in a conspiracy.
constitution			The fundamental law of a nation or state.
constructive			An act or condition assumed from other acts or conditions.
construe			To ascertain the meaning of language.
consummate			To complete.
contiguous			Adjoining; touching; bounded by.
contingent			Possible, but not assured; dependent upon some condition.
continuance			The adjournment or postponement of an action pending in a court.
contra			Against, opposed to; contrary.
contract			An agreement between two or more persons to do or not to do a particular thing.
conversion			Dealing with the personal property of another as if it were one's own, without right.
conveyance			An instrument transferring title to land.
conviction			Generally, the result of a criminal trial which ends in a judgment or sentence that the defendant is guilty as charged.
co-operative (also cooperative)			A cooperative is a voluntary organization of persons with a common interest, formed and operated along democratic lines for the purpose of supplying services at cost to its members and other patrons, who contribute both capital and business.
corroborate			To strengthen; to add weight by additional evidence.
counterclaim			A claim presented by a defendant in opposition to or deduction from the claim of the plaintiff.
county			Political subdivision of a state.
covenant			Agreement.
credible			Worthy of belief.
creditor			A person to whom a debt is owing by another person, called the "debtor".
criterion (sing.) criteria (pl.)			A means or tests for judging; a standard or standards.

124

	SIMPLIFIED	ANNIVERSARY	
damages			A monetary compensation, which may be recovered in the courts by any person who has suffered loss, or injury, whether to his person, property or rights through the unlawful act or omission or negligence of another.
de facto			In fact; actually but without legal authority.
de jure			Of right; legitimate; lawful.
de minimis			Very small or trifling.
de novo			Anew; afresh; a second time.
debt			A specified sum of money owing to one person from another, including not only the obligation of the debtor to pay, but the right of the creditor to receive and enforce payment.
decedent			A dead person.
decision			A judgment or decree pronounced by a court in determination of a case.
decree			An order of the court, determining the rights of all parties to a suit.
deed			A writing containing a contract sealed and delivered; particularly to convey real property.
default			The failure to fulfill a duty, observe a promise, discharge an obligation, or perform an agreement.

	SIMPLIFIED	ANNIVERSARY	
defendant			The person defending or denying; the party against whom relief or recovery is sought in an action or suit.
defraud			To practice fraud; to cheat or trick.
delegate			(v.) To entrust to the care or management of another.
demur (v.) demurrer (n.)			(v.) To dispute the sufficiency in law of the pleading of the other side.
demurrage			In maritime law, it means, the sum fixed or allowed as remuneration to the owners of a ship for the detention of their vessel beyond the number of days allowed for loading and unloading or for sailing; also used in railroad terminology.
denial			A form of pleading; refusing to admit the truth of a statement, charge, etc.
deposition			Testimony given under oath outside of court for use in court or for the purpose of obtaining information in preparation for trial of a case.
deponent			One who gives under oath testimony which is reduced to writing.
deterioration			A degeneration such as from decay, corrosion or disintegration.

	SIMPLIFIED	ANNIVERSARY	
detriment			Any loss or harm to person or property.
deviation			A turning aside.
devise			A gift of real property by the last will and testament of the donor.
dictum (sing.) dicta (pl.)			Any statements made by the court in an opinion concerning some rule of law not necessarily involved nor essential to the determination of the case.
disaffirm			To repudiate.
dismiss			In an action or suit, it means to dispose of the case without any further consideration or hearing.
dissent			To denote disagreement of one or more judges of a court with the decision passed by the majority upon a case before them.
docket			(n.) A formal record, entered in brief, of the proceedings in a court.
doctrine			A rule, principle, theory of law.
domicile			That place where a man has his true, fixed and permanent home to which whenever he is absent he has the intention of returning.
draft			(n.) A commercial paper ordering payment of money drawn by one person on another.
drawee			The person who is requested to pay the money.
drawer			The person who draws the commercial paper and addresses it to the drawee.
duress			Use of force to compel performance or non-performance of an act.

	SIMPLIFIED	ANNIVERSARY	
easement			A liberty, privilege, or advantage without profit, in the lands of another.
egress			Act or right of going out or leaving; emergence.
ejusdem generis			Of the same kind, class or nature. A rule used in the construction of language in a legal document.
embezzlement			To steal; to appropriate fraudulently to one's own use property entrusted to one's care.
enact			To make into a law.
endorsement			Act of writing one's name on the back of a note, bill or similar written instrument.
enjoin			To require a person, by writ of injunction from a court of equity, to perform or to abstain or desist from some act.
entirety			The whole; that which the law considers as one whole, and not capable of being divided into parts.
enumerated			Mentioned specifically; designated.
enure			To operate or take effect.

	SIMPLIFIED	ANNIVERSARY	
equity			In its broadest sense, this term denotes the spirit and the habit of fairness, justness, and right dealing which regulate the conduct of men.
error			A mistake of law, or the false or irregular application of law as will nullify the judicial proceedings.
escrow			A deed, bond or other written engagement, delivered to a third person, to be delivered by him only upon the performance or fulfillment of some condition.
estate			The interest which any one has in lands, or in any other subject of property.
estop			To stop, bar, or impede.
estoppel			A rule of law which prevents a man from alleging or denying a fact, because of his own previous act.
et al. (alii)			And others.
et seq. (sequential)			And the following.
et ux. (uxor)			And wife.
evidence			Documents or testimony of witnesses which tend to prove or disprove any matter in question, usually submitted to a jury to enable them to decide.

	SIMPLIFIED	ANNIVERSARY	
ex contractu ex delicto			In law, rights and causes of action are divided into two classes, those arising *ex contractu* (from a contract) and those arising *ex delicto* (from a delict or tort).
ex officio			From office; by virtue of the office.
ex parte			On one side only; by or for one.
ex post facto			After the fact.
ex rel. (relations)			Upon relation or information.
exception			An objection upon a matter of law to a decision made, either before or after judgment by a court.
executor (male) executrix (female)			A person who has been appointed by will to execute the will.
executory			That which is yet to be executed or performed.
exempt			To release from some liability to which others are subject.
exoneration			The removal of a burden, charge or duty.

F

	SIMPLIFIED	ANNIVERSARY	
f.a.s.			"Free alongside ship"; delivery at dock for ship named.
f.o.b.			"Free on board"; seller will deliver to car, truck, vessel, or other conveyance by which goods are to be transported, without expense or risk of loss to the buyer or consignee.
fabricate			To construct; to invent a false story.
factor			A commercial agent.
feasance			The doing of an act.
felony			Generally, a criminal offense that may be punished by death or imprisonment for more than one year as differentiated from a misdemeanor.
feme sole			A single woman.
fiduciary			A person who is invested with rights and powers to be exercised for the benefit of another person.
fieri facias			A writ of execution commanding the sheriff to levy and collect the amount of a judgment from the goods and chattels of the judgment debtor.
fiscal			Relating to accounts or the management of revenue.

	SIMPLIFIED	ANNIVERSARY	
foreclosure (sale)			A sale of mortgaged property to obtain satisfaction of the mortgage out of the sale proceeds.
forfeiture			A penalty, a fine.
forgery			Fabricating or producing falsely, counterfeited.
fortuitous			Accidental.
forum			A court of justice; a place of jurisdiction.
fraud			Deception; trickery.
fungible			Of such kind or nature that one specimen or part may be used in the place of another.

G

	SIMPLIFIED	ANNIVERSARY	
garnishment			A legal process to reach the money or effects of a defendant, in the possession or control of a third person.
garnishee			Person garnished.
grant			To agree to; convey, especially real property.
grantee			The person to whom a grant is made.
grantor			The person by whom a grant is made.
gratuitous			Given without a return, compensation or consideration.
guaranty			(n.) A promise to answer for the payment of some debt, or the performance of some duty, in case of the failure of another person, who, in the first instance, is liable for such payment or performance.
guilty			Establishment of the fact that one has committed a breach of conduct; especially a violation of law.

H

	SIMPLIFIED	ANNIVERSARY	
habeas corpus			You have the body; the name given to a variety of writs, having for their object to bring a party before a court or judge for decision as to whether such person is being lawfully held prisoner.
habendum			In conveyancing; it is the clause in a deed conveying land which defines the extent of ownership to be held by the grantee.
hearing			A proceeding whereby the arguments of the interested parties are heard.
hearsay			A type of testimony given by a witness who relates, not what he knows personally, but what others have told him, or what he has heard said by others.
heir			Generally, one who inherits property, real or personal.
hypothesis			A supposition, assumption, or theory.

I

	SIMPLIFIED	ANNIVERSARY	
i.e. (Id est)			That is.
ib., or ibid. (ibidem)			In the same place; used to refer to a legal reference previously cited to avoid repeating the entire citation.
illicit			Prohibited; unlawful.
illusory			Deceiving by false appearance.
immunity			Exemption.
impeach			To accuse, to dispute.
impediments			Disabilities, or hindrances.
implead			To sue or prosecute by due course of law.
implied			Not expressly stated; inferential.
imputed			Attributed or charged to.
in toto			In the whole; completely.
inchoate			Imperfect; unfinished.
incompetent			One who is incapable of caring for his own affairs because he is mentally deficient or undeveloped.
incumbrance			Generally a claim, lien, charge or liability attached to and binding real property.
indemnify			To secure against loss or damage; also, to make reimbursement to one for a loss already incurred by him.

	SIMPLIFIED	ANNIVERSARY	
indemnity			An agreement to reimburse another person in case of an anticipated loss falling upon him.
indicia			Signs; indications.
indictment			An accusation in writing found and presented by a grand jury charging that a person has committed a crime.
indorse			To write a name on the back of a legal paper or document generally, a negotiable instrument.
information			A formal accusation of crime made by a prosecuting attorney.
infra			Below, under; this word occurring by itself in a publication refers the reader to a future part of the publication.
ingress			The act of going into.
injunction			A writ or order by the court requiring a person generally, to do or to refrain from doing an act.
insolvent			The condition of a person who is unable to pay his debts.
instruction			A direction given by the judge to the jury concerning the law of the case.
interim			In the meantime; time intervening.
interlocutory			Temporary, not final; something intervening between the commencement and the end of a suit which decides some point or matter, but is not a final decision of the whole controversy.
interrogatories			A series of formal written questions used in the examination of a party or a witness usually prior to a trial.
intestate			A person who dies without a will.
inure			To result, to take effect.
ipso facto			By the fact itself; by the mere fact.
issue			(n.) The disputed point or question in a case.

13

131

	SIMPLIFIED	ANNIVERSARY	
jeopardy			Danger, hazard, peril.
joinder			Joining; uniting with another person in some legal steps or proceeding.
joint			United; combined.
judgment			The official decision of a court of justice.
judicial or judiciary			Relating to or connected with the administration of justice.
jurisdiction			The authority to hear and determine controversies between parties.
jurisprudence			The philosophy of law.
jury			A body of persons legally selected to inquire into any matter of fact, and to render their verdict according to the evidence.
jurat			The clause written at the foot of an affidavit, stating when, where and before whom such affidavit was sworn.

	SIMPLIFIED	ANNIVERSARY	
laches			The failure to diligently assert a right, which results in a refusal to allow relief.
landlord and tenant			A phrase used to denote the legal relation existing between the owner and occupant of real estate.
larceny			Stealing personal property belonging to another.
latent			Hidden; that which does not appear on the face of a thing.
lease			A contract by which one conveys real estate for a limited time usually for a specified rent; personal property also may be leased.
legislation			The act of enacting laws.
legitimate			Lawful.
lessee			One to whom a lease is given.
lessor			One who grants a lease.
levy			A collecting or exacting by authority.
liable			Responsible; bound or obligated in law or equity.
libel			(v.) To defame or injure a person's reputation by a published writing.
libel			(n.) The initial pleading on the part of the plaintiff in an admiralty proceeding.

	SIMPLIFIED	ANNIVERSARY	
lien			A hold or claim which one person has upon the property of another as a security for some debt or charge.
liquidated			Fixed; settled.
lis pendens			A pending suit.
literal			According to the language.
litigant			A party to a lawsuit.
litigation			A judicial controversy.
locus			A place.

	SIMPLIFIED	ANNIVERSARY	
malice			The doing of a wrongful act intentionally without just cause or excuse.
mandamus			The name of a writ issued by a court to enforce the performance of some public duty.
mandatory			(adj.) Containing a command.
marshalling			Arranging or disposing of in order.
maxim			An established principle or proposition.
ministerial			That which involves obedience to instruction, but demands no special discretion, judgment or skill.
misappropriate			Dealing fraudulently with property entrusted to one.
misdemeanor			A crime less than a felony and punishable by a fine or imprisonment for less than one year.
misrepresentation			An untrue representation of facts.
mitigate			To make or become less severe, harsh.
moot			(adj.) Unsettled, undecided, not necessary to be decided.
mortgage			A conveyance of property upon condition, as security for the payment of a debt or the performance of a duty, and to become void upon payment or performance according to the stipulated terms.

	SIMPLIFIED	ANNIVERSARY	
mortgagee			A person to whom property is mortgaged.
mortgagor			One who gives a mortgage.
motion			In legal proceedings, a "motion" is an application, either written or oral, addressed to the court by a party to an action or a suit requesting the ruling of the court on a matter of law.
mutuality			Reciprocation.

	SIMPLIFIED	ANNIVERSARY	
negligence			The failure to exercise that degree of care which an ordinarily prudent person would exercise under like circumstances.
negotiable (instrument)			Any instrument obligating the payment of money which is transferable from one person to another by endorsement and delivery or by delivery only.
negotiate			To transact business; to transfer a negotiable instrument; to seek agreement for the amicable disposition of a controversy or case.
nolle prosequi			A formal entry upon the record, by the plaintiff in a civil suit or the prosecuting officer in a criminal action, by which he declares that he "will no further prosecute" the case.
nolo contendere			The name of a plea in a criminal action, having the same effect as a plea of guilty; but not constituting a direct admission of guilt.
nominal			Not real or substantial.
novation			The substitution of a new debt or obligation for an existing one.
nunc pro tunc			A phrase applied to acts allowed to be done after the time when they should be done, with a retroactive effect.

17

	SIMPLIFIED	ANNIVERSARY	
order			A rule or regulation; every direction of a court or judge made or entered in writing but not including a judgment.
ordinance			Generally, a rule established by authority; also commonly used to designate the legislative acts of a municipal corporation.

	SIMPLIFIED	ANNIVERSARY	
object			(v.) To oppose as improper or illegal and referring the question of its propriety or legality to the court.
obligation			A legal duty, by which a person is bound to do or not to do a certain thing.
obligee			The person to whom an obligation is owed.
obligor			The person who is to perform the obligation.
offer			(v.) To present for acceptance or rejection.
offer			(n.) A proposal to do a thing, usually a proposal to make a contract.
offset			A deduction.
opinion			The statement by a judge of the decision reached in a case, giving the law as applied to the case and giving reasons for the judgment; also, a belief or view.
option			The exercise of the power of choice; also a privilege existing in one person, for which he has paid money, which gives him the right to buy or sell real or personal property at a given price within a specified time.

P

	SIMPLIFIED	ANNIVERSARY		
parol			Oral or verbal.	
parity			Equality in purchasing power between the farmer and other segments of the economy.	
partition			A legal division of real or personal property between one or more owners.	
partnership			An association of two or more persons to carry on as co-owners a business for profit.	
patent			(adj.) Evident.	
patent			(n.) A grant of some privilege, property, or authority, made by the government or sovereign of a country to one or more individuals.	
pecuniary			Monetary.	
penultimate			Next to the last.	
per curiam			A phrase used in the report of a decision to distinguish an opinion of the whole court from an opinion written by any one judge.	
per se			In itself; taken alone.	
peremptory			Imperative; absolute.	
perjury			To lie or state falsely under oath.	

	SIMPLIFIED	ANNIVERSARY	
perpetuity			Perpetual existence; also the quality or condition of an estate limited so that it will not take effect or vest within the period fixed by law.
personalty			Short term for personal property.
petition			An application in writing for an order of the court, stating the circumstances upon which it is founded and, requesting any order or other relief from a court.
plaintiff			A person who brings a court action.
plea			A pleading in a suit or action.
pleadings			Formal allegations made by the parties of their respective claims and defenses, for the judgment of the court.
pledge			A deposit of personal property as a security for the performance of an act.
pledgee			The party to whom goods are delivered in pledge.
pledgor			The party delivering goods in pledge.
plenary			Full; complete.
precept			An order, warrant, or writ issued to an officer or body of officers, commanding him or them to do some act within the scope of his or their powers.
preponderance			Outweighing.

	SIMPLIFIED	ANNIVERSARY	
prima facie			At first sight.
principal			The source of authority or rights; a person primarily liable as differentiated from "principle" as a primary or basic doctrine.
pro rata			Proportionally.
probate			Relating to proof, especially to the proof of wills.
procedure			In law, this term generally denotes rules which are established by the Federal, State or local Governments regarding the types of pleading and courtroom practice which must be followed by the parties involved in a criminal or civil case.
proclamation			A public notice by an official of some order, intended action, or state of facts.
promissory (note)			A promise in writing to pay a specified sum at an expressed time, or on demand, or at sight, to a named person, or to his order, or bearer.
proprietary			(adj.) Relating or pertaining to ownership; usually a single owner.
prosecute			To carry on an action or other judicial proceeding; to proceed against a person criminally.
proviso			A limitation or condition in a legal instrument.
proximate			Immediate; nearest.
punitive			Relating to punishment.

	SIMPLIFIED	ANNIVERSARY		
q				
quash	⊢	⊢	To make void.	
quasi	⊖	⊖	As if; as it were.	
quid pro quo	⫫	⫫	Something for something; the giving of one valuable thing for another.	
quitclaim	∽∽	∽∽	(v.) To release or relinquish claim or title to, especially in deeds to realty.	

	SIMPLIFIED	ANNIVERSARY	
R			
ratify	⌒	⌒	To approve and sanction.
realty	⌒	⌒	A brief term for real property.
rebut	2	2	To contradict; to refute, especially by evidence and arguments.
receiver	2	2	A person who is appointed by the court to receive, and hold in trust, property in litigation.
reciprocal	⌒	⌒	Mutual.
recoupment	⌒	⌒	To keep back or get something which is due; also, it is the right of a defendant to have a deduction from the amount of the plaintiff's damages because the plaintiff has not fulfilled his part of the same contract.
redeem	⌒	⌒	To release an estate or article from mortgage or pledge by paying the debt for which it stood as security.
referee	⌒	⌒	A person to whom a cause pending in a court is referred by the court, to take testimony, hear the parties, and report thereon to the court.
referendum	⌒	⌒	A method of submitting an important legislative or administrative matter to a direct vote of the people.
remand	⌒	⌒	To send a case back to the lower court from which it came, for further proceedings.

	SIMPLIFIED	ANNIVERSARY	
replevin			An action to recover goods or chattels wrongfully taken or detained.
reply (replication)			Generally, a reply is what the plaintiff or other person who has instituted proceedings says in answer to the defendant's case.
res judicata			A thing judicially acted upon or decided.
rescind (rescission)			To avoid or cancel a contract.
respondent			A defendant in a proceeding in chancery or admiralty; also, the person who contends against the appeal in a case.
restitution			In equity, it is the restoration of both parties to their original condition (when practicable), upon the rescission of a contract for fraud or similar cause.
retroactive (retrospective)			Looking back; effective as of a prior time.
reversed			A term used by appellate courts to indicate that the decision of the lower court in the case before it has been set aside.
revoke			To recall or cancel.
riparian (rights)			The rights of a person owning land containing or bordering on a water course or other body of water, such as lakes and rivers.

	SIMPLIFIED	ANNIVERSARY	
sale			A contract whereby the ownership of property is transferred from one person to another for a sum of money or for any consideration.
sanction			A penalty or punishment provided as a means of enforcing obedience to a law; also, an authorization.
satisfaction			The discharge of an obligation by paying a party what is due to him; or what is awarded to him, by the judgment of a court or otherwise.
scienter			Knowingly; also, it is used in pleading to denote the defendant's guilty knowledge.
scintilla			A spark; also the least particle.
security			Indemnification; the term is applied to an obligation, such as a mortgage or deed of trust, given by a debtor to insure the payment or performance of his debt, by furnishing the creditor with a resource to be used in case of the debtor's failure to fulfill the principal obligation.
sentence			The judgment formally pronounced by the court or judge upon the defendant after his conviction in a criminal prosecution.
set-off			A claim or demand which one party in an action credits against the claim of the opposing party.
situs			Location.

	SIMPLIFIED	ANNIVERSARY	
sovereign			A person, body, or state in which independent and supreme authority is vested.
stare decisis			To follow decided cases.
statute			An act of the legislature.
statute of limitation			A statute limiting the time to bring an action after the right of action has arisen.
stay			To hold in abeyance an order of a court.
stipulation			Any agreement made by opposing attorneys regulating any matter incidental to the proceedings or trial.
subordination (agreement)			An agreement making one's rights inferior to or of a lower rank than another's.
subornation			The crime of procuring a person to lie or to make false statements to a court.
subpoena			A writ or order directed to a person, and requiring his attendance at a particular time and place to testify as a witness.
subpoena duces tecum			A subpoena used, not only for the purpose of compelling witnesses to attend in court, but also requiring them to bring with them books or documents which may be in their possession, and which may tend to elucidate the subject matter of the trial.

	SIMPLIFIED	ANNIVERSARY	
subrogation			The substituting of one for another as a creditor, the new creditor succeeding to the former's rights.
subsidy			A government grant to assist a private enterprise deemed advantageous to the public.
suit			Any civil proceeding by a person or persons against another or others in a court of justice by which the plaintiff pursues the remedies afforded him by law.
summons			A notice to a defendant that an action against him has been commenced and requiring him to appear in court and answer the complaint.
supra			Above; this word occurring by itself in a book refers the reader to a previous part of the book.
surety			A person who binds himself for the payment of a sum of money, or for the performance of something else, for another.
surplusage			Extraneous or unnecessary matter.
survivorship			A term used when a person becomes entitled to property by reason of his having survived another person who had an interest in the property.
syllabus			A note prefixed to a report, especially a case, giving a brief statement of the court's ruling on different issues of the case.

T

	SIMPLIFIED	ANNIVERSARY	
tenant			One who holds or possesses lands by any kind of right or title; also, one who has the temporary use and occupation of real property owned by another person (landlord), the duration and terms of his tenancy being usually fixed by an instrument called "a lease".
tender			An offer of money; an expression of willingness to perform a contract according to its terms.
term			When used with reference to a court, it signifies the period of time during which the court holds a session, usually of several weeks or months duration.
testamentary			Pertaining to a will or the administration of a will.
testator (male) testatrix (female)			One who makes or has made a testament or will.
testify (testimony)			To give evidence under oath as a witness.
to wit			That is to say; namely.
tort			Wrong; injury to the person.
transitory			Passing from place to place.
trial			The examination of a cause, civil or criminal, before a judge who has jurisdiction over it, according to the laws of the land.
trust			A right of property, real or personal, held by one party for the benefit of another.

U

	SIMPLIFIED	ANNIVERSARY	
ultra vires			Acts beyond the scope and power of a corporation, association, etc.
unilateral			One-sided; obligation upon, or act of one party.

V

	SIMPLIFIED	ANNIVERSARY	
vacate	↗	↗	To set aside; to move out.
variance	↗	↗	A discrepancy or disagreement between two instruments or two aspects of the same case, which by law should be consistent.
vendee	↗	↗	A purchaser or buyer.
vendor	↗	↗	The person who transfers property by sale, particularly real estate; the term "seller" is used more commonly for one who sells personal property.
venue	↗	↗	The place at which an action is tried, generally based on locality or judicial district in which an injury occurred or a material fact happened.
verdict	↗	↗	The formal decision or finding of a jury.
verify	↗	↗	To confirm or substantiate by oath.
vest	↗	↗	To accrue to.
void	↗	↗	Having no legal force or binding effect.

W

	SIMPLIFIED	ANNIVERSARY	
waiver	↗	↗	The intentional or voluntary relinquishment of a known right.
warrant (warranty)	↗	↗	(v.) To promise that a certain fact or state of facts, in relation to the subject matter, is, or shall be, as it is represented to be.
warrant	↗	↗	(n.) A writ issued by a judge, or other competent authority, addressed to a sheriff, or other officer, requiring him to arrest the person therein named, and bring him before the judge or court, to answer or be examined regarding the offense with which he is charged.
writ	↗	↗	An order or process issued in the name of the sovereign or in the name of a court or judicial officer, commanding the performance or nonperformance of some act.

www.ingramcontent.com/pod-product-compliance
Lightning Source LLC
Chambersburg PA
CBHW082205300426
44117CB00016B/2683